VOTES FOR WOMEN

VOTES FOR WOMEN

CHELTENHAM
AND THE
COTSWOLDS

SUE JONES

FOREWORD BY DAME FELICITY LOTT

The History Press

In memory of my father, Ron West, who passed on his love of local history, and of Aunty Edna who told me intriguing stories of her encounters with suffragettes.

First published 2018

The History Press
The Mill, Brimscombe Port
Stroud, Gloucestershire, GL5 2QG
www.thehistorypress.co.uk

British Library Cataloguing in Publication Data.
A catalogue record for this book is available from the British Library.

ISBN 978 0 7509 8277 1

Typesetting and origination by The History Press
Printed and bound in Great Britain by TJ International Ltd, Padstow, Cornwall

CONTENTS

Acknowledgements

I am very grateful to the archivists and librarians in Cheltenham, Gloucester, Cirencester and Stroud, and at the Museum of London and the Women's Library, LSE: they have all been unfailingly helpful with advice and assistance with my technical shortcomings! The archivists at both Cheltenham Ladies' College and North London Collegiate School kindly spent much time in searching out relevant material: in turn, I hope they can use some of the information I have uncovered about their ex-pupils and staff.

Many personal friends have offered encouragement, as have a number of people I have met through local history links who have also pointed me towards other sources. I should particularly like to thank Hilary Simpson, Linda Viner and Elaine and Geoff North. Neela Mann has been invaluable in her support, practical help and detailed advice. Most of all, my husband Paul deserves huge thanks for his work on the illustrations, IT advice – and his forbearance!

FOREWORD

As I cycled daily to Pate's Grammar School for Girls from my home in Alstone Croft, I had no idea that a cyclist from the same road was a witness to a dramatic part of the women's suffrage story in Cheltenham. The grand house nearby, Alstone Lawn, was long gone by the time my parents bought the small house where I grew up. In 1913 it was set on fire by two members of the suffragette movement and the incident was reported by a man cycling home from work to Alstone Croft.

While Sue and I were at school together, we never learned about the women's suffrage campaign, let alone any bits of the local story. So I have found it fascinating to find out about it and to be able to relate many parts to the area which I knew when I was young. I am so pleased to be invited to write this foreword: Sue and I took different paths, she to be a History teacher and I to be a singer, but we have remained friends all our lives.

Now we have a record number of women MPs who all have reason to be grateful to the women who protested and fought so bravely over 100 years ago against the tyranny of men!

Dame Felicity Lott
July 2017

Introduction

February 2018 sees the centenary of the first granting of the parliamentary vote to women in Britain. This was a momentous step for women, but only for some. The vote was limited to those women over 30 who were householders, the wives of householders, occupiers of property with an annual rent of more than £5 or graduates. All men over 21 were given the right to vote in the same Act; in fact, it was aimed more at them than at the women. The Act meant that not all the women who had campaigned so hard for the vote would have been granted it.

This book is an attempt to show how the local women's suffrage movement, in all its fragmented parts, developed. Cheltenham was the centre of activities, with 'outreach' work to Tewkesbury and surrounding areas. However, Cirencester and Stroud had their own stories although again Cheltenham often provided the initial spur to activity. I say 'fragmented parts' because it is often assumed that the suffragettes were the sum total of the movement. That could not be further from the truth and in this book I aim to show the true breadth of activity, of the suffragettes (the militants) and the suffragists (the constitutionalists).

Most researchers into women's suffrage in the early twentieth century are faced by a lack of branch and membership records. This is particularly so for the militants because many records were destroyed in order to stop them falling into the hands of the police. Reliance on newspaper accounts, both local and organisational, is necessary. However, the discovery in Gloucestershire Archives of an apparently insignificant book of signatures has transformed my study. This dusty and crumbling book contains the signatures of both leaders and foot-soldiers of the local movement in 1912. It was presented to the local MP James Agg-Gardner as thanks for his sponsoring of a women's suffrage bill in the Commons. By cross-referencing to the 1911 census and other sources, I have been able to fill out the profiles of many of those involved and to discover many women, and men, who would otherwise have

The 1912 book of thanks to James Agg-Gardner, MP for Cheltenham, for his support for women's suffrage. The signatures of nearly 500 men and women transformed the picture of supporters in the area. (D5130/6/6, Gloucestershire Archives)

remained hidden. So much richness and detail has been added to what would have been a much more fragmentary picture.

My interest in the women's suffrage movement was sparked by the stories an elderly aunt told me when I was a child. She had been a student at Stockwell Training College, London, from 1912–14 and had witnessed some of the suffragette scenes and been in an alleged bomb scare at a church (though I think she exaggerated all this for effect!). She had also shared a dormitory with another girl from Derby, as she was, and this girl was from a strong suffragette family.[1] There was a hint that my aunt may have accompanied her to a meeting as the students were not allowed out alone.

---

1   This was Winnie Wheeldon who, with her mother and husband, was in 1917 imprisoned for attempting to poison Lloyd George as part of their pacifist agitation. There is currently an attempt to clear their names as it seems that they were 'set up' by a government agent.

When I took early retirement from teaching, I decided to pursue this interest and studied the movement in the North East where I was then living. This involved delving into the lives of women in mining communities and, in contrast, of those in wealthy merchant families in Newcastle. Returning to my home area of the Cotswolds a few years ago, I was keen to see what the movement was like here. Just as I had assumed that the male-oriented social and economic atmosphere of the North East would snuff out the women's movement, I assumed that the 'gentility' of Cheltenham might not be conducive to feminism. I have been proved wrong on both scores! While the anti-suffrage movement was probably better organised than in the North East, particularly in Cirencester, it was still possible for women to cause a stir.

And women did cause a stir! The genteel patina of Cheltenham was rocked by demonstrations, rowdy meetings and defiance of the law. Cirencester women battled against the forces of the Bathurst family and its local political dominance and, in Stroud, the MP's antagonism to women's suffrage was challenged. In smaller centres such as Winchcombe, Tewkesbury and Nailsworth, women emerged who were prepared to defy the convention that only men occupied public political spaces. Spirited and determined women fought on a number of fronts and their stories are fascinating. But the role of supportive men is often forgotten in the story of women's suffrage and they too emerge in the following pages.

Glossary and Abbreviations

Women's suffrage groups:
Actresses' Franchise League (AFL)
Conservative and Unionist Women's Franchise Association (CUWFA) – suffragist
National Union of Women's Suffrage Societies (NUWSS or WSS) – suffragist
Women's Freedom League (WFL) – suffragette breakaway from WSPU
Women's Social and Political Union (WSPU) – suffragette
Men's Political Union (MPU)

Newspapers and Journals:
The Common Cause (CC) – NUWSS paper
The Conservative and Unionist Women's Franchise Review (CUWFR)
The Vote – WFL paper
Votes for Women (VFW) – WSPU paper
The Suffragette – WSPU paper after 1912

Cheltenham Chronicle and Gloucestershire Graphic (CCGG)
Cheltenham Chronicle (Chronicle)
Cheltenham Looker-On (Looker-On)
Cheltenham Examiner (Examiner)
Gloucestershire Echo (Echo)
Wiltshire and Glos Standard (Standard)
Stroud News
Stroud Journal
Gloucester Journal
Gloucester Citizen

Other abbreviations

Independent Labour Party (ILP)

Cheltenham Ladies' College (CLC)

Archives

Suffragette Fellowship Archive, Museum of London (SF Archive)

SELECT BIBLIOGRAPHY

Elizabeth Crawford: *The Women's Suffrage Movement: A Reference Guide. 1866–1928* (London; UCL Press, 1999)

Elizabeth Crawford: *The Women's Suffrage Movement in Britain and Ireland* (London; Routledge, 2005)

Roger Fulford: *Votes for Women* ((London; Faber & Faber, 1957)

Jill Liddington: *Rebel Girls* (London; Virago, 2006)

Jill Liddington: *Vanishing the Vote* (Manchester; MUP, 2014)

Sylvia Pankhurst: *The Suffragette Movement* (London; Virago, 1977)

Martin Pugh: *The March of the Women* (Oxford; OUP, 2000)

Martin Pugh: *The Pankhursts* (London; Penguin, 2001)

1

'The Suffragette Outrage at Cheltenham'

(Gloucester Journal, 27 December 1913)

'ALSTONE LAWN SET ON FIRE. UNKNOWN WOMEN ARRESTED ON SUSPICION.' *Gloucestershire Echo,* 22 December 1913

'ARSON IN CHELTENHAM … UNKNOWN WOMEN ARRESTED ON SUSPICION.' *Cheltenham Chronicle,* 27 December 1913

These headlines are of the kind which many associate with the struggle for women's suffrage and they would appear to suggest that Cheltenham was in the grip of a wave of suffragette 'terrorism' which characterised the struggle elsewhere. This is wrong on two counts. Firstly, the incident at Alstone Lawn was an isolated one, perpetrated by outside itinerant fire-raisers. Secondly, the campaign for women's suffrage included non-militant groups who were at least as important as the militants.

Nevertheless, headlines like this expressed the fear and outrage among many sections of society and were frequently articulated by the local and national press. So what actually happened and how was it reported?

In the early morning of Sunday, 21 December 1913, a fire was reported to the fire station in St James' Square and to Cheltenham police. Alstone Lawn, a large but empty house in seven acres of grounds on the corner of Gloucester Road and Alstone Lane, was ablaze. The man who had seen flames darting from the roof was a gasworker, Edward Batson, who was cycling home to Alstone Croft from his job at the gasworks in Gloucester Road. He raced to the fire station in St James' Square to raise the alarm. Such was the concern that both divisions of the brigade were ordered out and twenty men arrived to find the police already there. The house and grounds were surrounded by an eight-foot wall, some of which had an additional fence on the top and so they had to break into the stable yard and then into the house. The source of the fire was located in the wooden staircase which ran from the bottom to the top of the building. The hydrants were quickly employed, so the services of the engine were not needed and the fire was brought under control in half an hour. At 8.30 a.m., Fire Officer Such decided that the brigade could leave, though one man together with a number of police officers remained at the premises. A big hole had been made in the roof, damage was estimated at £300–400 and it was later decided that the house should be pulled down and the estate sold in small lots for further development.

What of the culprits? It was quickly established that the cause was arson, as a two-gallon oil can, still wet with paraffin, was found near the seat of the fire and it appeared that there were oil marks on the wallpaper nearby. A window to the conservatory on the ground floor was found open and, as the firemen and policemen had not used it, it was assumed that this was the method of entry. This theory was reinforced by the discovery of imprints of stockinged feet, one with a prominent large toe, on the floor of the same room. Suffrage literature was found in the grounds of the house. By 9.30 a.m., two women coming from the direction of Arle and the Cross Hands Inn were arrested in the Tewkesbury Road by Sergeant

Alstone Lawn, the magnificent though deserted house, set on fire in December 1913 by two suffragettes. (The Cheltenham Trust and Cheltenham Borough Council)

The Cheltenham firemen based at St James' Square fire station, who dealt with the blaze at Alstone Lawn. (*Cheltenham Chronicle and Gloucestershire Graphic*, 6 December 1913)

Welchman, whose suspicion was aroused by a strong smell of paraffin. It was also alleged that they had been seen by a policeman in the area of Alstone Lawn about half an hour before the fire was discovered. At the police station, paraffin was found on their stockings, boots and on the shorter woman's cloak. Neither woman was prepared to give her name or address, they protested against 'man-made laws', began a hunger-and-thirst strike and were locked up.

At the police court appearance on the Monday morning, the women were labelled 'Red' and 'Black'. As well as the unusually good photograph we have of them coming out of the police station, we have the details circulated by the police:

When arrested, one of the women, whose age is 21 or 22, and who stands 5ft 1in or 5ft 2in., was wearing a navy blue skirt with white silk blouse, a dark grey rainproof coat, and a navy blue felt hat, with silk band. She was wearing a pair of black shoes, grey gloves, and a blue woollen scarf. This woman, who is well-built, has brown hair and blue eyes, and a full face.

The second prisoner is 23 years of age and about 5ft. 3in. in height. She has a small face, with brown hair and eyes. She is very slightly built, and has prominent teeth. When apprehended she was wearing a navy blue dress, with lace on the sleeves, a red 'Teddy-bear' cloth coat (with large black buttons, a turned-down collar, and a strap at the back), a red felt hat with fur band, a black veil, and sized four Derby shoes.

Both were therefore well-dressed in 'respectable' clothes and in no way were trying to avoid notice. Much was made of their appearance and demeanour in the press, the fact that they seemed to have been in high spirits when they arrived in court ('they bounced into the box evidently in a very happy frame of mind with themselves', CCGG 27/12/13), that both had their hair loose (not a sign of 'respectability') and with some comments on who was the better-looking. The tone was of mild wonderment and, at the same time, disapproval. The local press did not report what *The Suffragette* newspaper said – that the police had refused to allow them shoes, stockings or hairpins, the former because they were allegedly needed in evidence,

Lilian Lenton and her accomplice Olive Wharry, coming out of Cheltenham Police Court after being found guilty of the fire at Alstone Lawn. (*Cheltenham Chronicle and Gloucestershire Graphic*, 27 December 1913)

as was the coat of one of them, the hairpins presumably as they could be used to self-harm or attack others.

One curious aspect of the case was that the charge which was made against them included the allegation that they intended to injure the owner of the property, Colonel B. de Sales la Terriere. This would not have held up in court if the case had been argued as the house had been empty since the death of the colonel's mother in September 1911, the contents had been sold at auction in May 1912 and the whole estate had been unsuccessfully put up for sale. The fact that the surrounding boarding fence was described as dilapidated in places added to the impression that the property was deserted and it was a typical target for the suffragettes, who never sought to hurt people, only property.

The women refused to answer to the 'male court' and were therefore remanded in custody. They left the police court in a taxi to the Midland Station to catch the train to Worcester, where they were to be held in gaol. Again, the local press commented on their appearance as they left the court, both barefoot and with their hair loose, and also on the fact that they were greeted by at least two lady sympathisers, one of whom, 'in a long brown coat', followed them to the station and was allowed by the police escorts to chat freely to them. It was noted that at both the police station and the railway station they attempted to hide their faces from photographers. One senses continuing disapproval but perhaps grudging admiration for their resolute courage from the *Gloucestershire Echo* and the *Cheltenham Chronicle and Gloucestershire Graphic*, but the *Gloucester Journal* was less forgiving. It spoke of 'dastardly' acts, 'nefarious work' and 'suffragette firebrands infesting the country'.

Throughout all the reporting, it was assumed that these women were suffragettes and certainly the evidence pointed in that direction. Apparently the fire chief had even sent one of the divisions back to the fire station when he had assessed the situation at Alstone Lawn, as fire brigades throughout the country had been warned always to leave some men on duty, it being believed that 'when Suffragettes intend to make a big attack on property by fire they will probably create a small fire elsewhere as a ruse whereby to detract the attention of the firefighters.' This was not the case here.

The two women, 'Red' and 'Black', were released from Worcester Gaol on 25 December under the terms of the 'Cat and Mouse' Act of April 1913. Officially the Prisoners' Temporary Discharge for Ill Health Act, it had been passed by a jittery government to prevent there being a suffragette death on their hands at a time when hunger strikes by the women prisoners had become a political embarrassment. Prisoners suffering from ill-health because of hunger/thirst strikes could be released on licence until they had recovered sufficiently to be imprisoned again. 'Red' and

A Home Office surveillance photograph of arsonist Lilian Lenton in prison, probably June 1913, before her Cheltenham offence. (Wikipedia, public domain)

'Black' were supposed to reappear at Cheltenham on Monday, 29 December but proved to be elusive 'mice', who went into hiding and whom the government and police 'cats' could not catch.[1]

It was, however, reported that fingerprints had been obtained and that it should soon be possible to identify the culprits. This seems to have been a reasonable assumption as, after the passing of the 'Cat and Mouse' Act, it had become more important for the police to be able to identify the 'mice' who had escaped or were evading recapture. Fingerprinting and covert photographing of prisoners were being developed and, in June 1913, when the young suffragette Lilian Lenton was in Armley Gaol (Leeds), a telegram was sent to the Home Office to ask whether,

---

1   There is a 1960 interview with Lilian Lenton in the BBC archives where she describes being driven from Cheltenham to a house in Birmingham on Christmas Day 1913, and managing to evade the Birmingham police who arrived too late to observe her escape. She had obviously forgotten that she had been in gaol in Worcester rather than in Cheltenham.

'in the Event of Liberation on Bail should photo and fingerprints be taken' (Liddington: *Rebel Girls*, p.280). The prompt response was 'Yes', and this is the photo which was undoubtedly taken of Lilian Lenton and which was later one of a strip of photographs circulated to police forces by the Home Office. She was evidently one of the two culprits. On 9 May 1914, the *Gloucester Journal* reported that she had been arrested at Birkenhead and steps were being taken to bring her before the Cheltenham bench for the Alstone Lawn attack, but her continued pattern of arrest, hunger-striking, temporary release and further escape prevented this ever happening and she was still legally a 'mouse' when the war broke out.

Lilian Lenton was, effectively, a professional itinerant arsonist for the Women's Social and Political Union (WSPU) as the suffragette organisation was officially known. She was involved in a number of high-profile attacks on property, notably Kew Gardens tea house. It was her near-death from septic pneumonia caused by force-feeding in Holloway Prison in February 1913 that had helped propel the government to pass the 'Cat and Mouse' Act. Some of the suffragettes undoubtedly embellished accounts of their activities in later years (and conversely some never spoke of them at all) but Lilian Lenton's 1960 interview for the BBC proudly

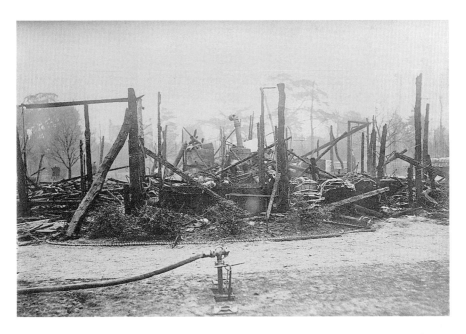

Kew Gardens teahouse after the fire caused by Lilian Lenton and Olive Wharry, February 1913. (Postcard, author's collection)

recalled that she had announced at WSPU headquarters in February 1913 that 'I didn't want to break more windows but that I did want to burn some buildings,' so long as 'it did not endanger human life other than our own' (transcript, Museum of London, Suffragette Fellowship collection). She recalled that 'my object was to burn two buildings a week'. What drew her to Cheltenham and Alstone Lawn cannot be known although her parents were living in Bristol at this stage, but she must somehow have acquired the knowledge of the empty property and one wonders whether this was via a very local informant.

It is likely that the other woman was Olive Wharry. She had been jointly charged with Lilian Lenton for the Kew Gardens fire and was responsible for a number of other incidents, sometimes going under the alias Joyce Locke or Phyllis North. The daughter of middle-class parents and a few years older than Lilian Lenton, she was at least as determined as her ultimately more famous companion and has left a revealing scrapbook, now in the British Library, of her time in Holloway Prison earlier in 1913. During this time, she purports to have been on hunger strike for thirty-one days and to have lost over two stone in weight.

The story of the Alstone Lawn incident is interesting in its own right, for the light it sheds on the effect of WSPU militancy on a local area and on aspects of the national campaign. However, two fascinating intersections with other parts of the Cheltenham women's suffrage movement occur in this story. When 'Red' and 'Black' were brought before the court in December 1913, on the bench was Alderman Margrett, who had proved himself to be a supporter of the women's suffrage cause over a number of years, but of the non-militant wing of the movement. This confrontation with women whose objective he supported, but whose methods he did not, must have tested his professionalism.

Perhaps more intriguing because he chose to put himself in that position, rather than found himself there as Alderman Margrett did, is the appearance in court in January 1914 of the Cheltenham solicitor Dr Earengey. He was a very prominent supporter of other women's suffrage organisations and his wife led the Women's Franchise League in Cheltenham. Much more will be said about them in later chapters. Dr Earengey was appearing for an agent of 'Red' and 'Black' to request the return of money and jewellery which had been taken from them on their arrest. He pointed out that it was acceptable that clothing and shoes might be needed for forensic purposes but saw no reason for the retention of the other items, particularly as the jewellery had belonged to the mother of one of them. He promised to hand over the money and articles to the women or to someone authorised to pass them on. However, he failed in his plea because he did not know the names or whereabouts of the women and had no proof of being appointed to act on their behalf. Superintendent Hopkins also made it clear that, if found guilty, the money found on them might be held against the costs of the trial or the damage to the property (*Gloucester Journal* 17/01/14).

The position of Dr Earengey was ambiguous – who was the 'agent' who had approached him to appear before the court? Had he fully considered how his appearance on behalf of the two women might be construed by his fellows in the non-militant movement? The last question is perhaps partly answered by the somewhat unusual, and perhaps unpremeditated, exchange between him and the chairman at the end of the proceedings:

> Dr Earengey: I would like to ask the indulgence of the Court one moment longer, and to say that so far as I am concerned in the application this morning, I appear simply as an advocate … I should like to add that, so far as I am concerned, I entirely reprobate the proceedings which have taken place, and which led to the arrest of the two women.
>
> Chairman: We don't doubt that.
>
> Dr Earengey: I wished to make that statement because sometimes one's attitude is misconstrued.

This statement attempted to clarify his position.

The drama of the fire at Alstone Lawn and its perpetrators was not typical of the women's suffrage movement in the Cotswolds, and it can be argued that the spectacular events had less overall impact on people's views than the unspectacular – although most of the press would wish to believe otherwise. Whichever is the case, in the course of exploring what happened in the area, one encounters women of great character and perseverance, and seams of activities and opinions of fascinating richness. It is these which are explored in the following chapters.

The National Context and Local Beginnings

As the new century dawned in 1900, there was much anticipation of new political directions. The embryonic Labour Party was in the process of being formed with the objective of getting working men's representatives in Parliament. Also, the women's suffrage movement was about to take a leap forward with the formation in 1903 of the Women's Social Political Union (WSPU). So, although in many ways, my decision to look at the local women's suffrage movement from 1900 might seem an arbitrary one, it has the merits of reflecting the national scene. In the case of Cheltenham, it reflects the fact that a women's suffrage society had just been re-formed and was slowly gaining support.

National anxieties

Yet these were not wholly optimistic times: the Boer War was bitterly dividing public opinion to the extent that political parties and many communities experienced real anguish. Revelations of army brutality and the setting up of British concentration camps caused opponents of the war to vent their disgust while those with a strong imperialist or nationalist belief tended to support British action. The two future leaders of the women's suffrage movement, Millicent Fawcett and Emmeline Pankhurst, were also on opposing sides. An example of the intensity of feeling is Mrs Pankhurst's youngest daughter, Adela, having a book thrown in her face at school because of her mother's criticism of British policy (Liddington: *Rebel Girls* p.2). In a town such as Cheltenham, with its strong army and colonial presence, these tensions were undoubtedly present.

The war also revealed dire statistics about the physical health of the nation: the army attracted many volunteers but approximately one third of them were rejected on grounds of slight stature or physical problems. This raised questions about working-class lifestyles, their economic well-being and, amongst some commentators, about the role of mothers in providing the nation with healthy young men (and women!). These questions about national poverty had been raised previously by investigators such as Charles Booth in London and Joseph Rowntree in York, but the politicians only really took notice when the impact of poverty on foreign/imperial policy became apparent. As a result, the years before the First World War saw the beginnings of the welfare state with the introduction of school medical inspections, free school meals, old age pensions and National Insurance to provide sickness benefit and unemployment benefit to some groups of workers.

This is important for understanding the debate about women's suffrage, as many of its opponents argued that a woman's role was clearly domestic; her energies should be concentrated on ensuring that she managed the household efficiently and wisely and brought up healthy children to serve their country. However, these arguments were clearly directed primarily at working-class women and few campaigners argued for the immediate enfranchisement of that group. The argument that women as 'angels of the home' contributed something different from men could be used to support both sides of the debate, either that this was where they should remain, or that they could bring their unique contribution to the realm of public affairs.

With the death of Queen Victoria in January 1901, the nation was also plunged into some uncertainty. Nevertheless, the whole tone of Edwardian England was still set by a consciousness of imperial glory and by a very wealthy elite who dominated society and, if they were male, politics. The campaigns of the women had to unsettle this cosy elite, and it is testimony to their success that they were able to break into some of these circles and recruit supporters from the aristocracy.

Women's position in society

There had been some progress in women's position in society in the last half of the nineteenth century. Some had been legal progress, such as the right to divorce (1857), the right to retain ownership of her own property gained either before or after marriage through the Married Women's Property Act of 1884, and limited rights for married women over their children in 1886. Some were social: at long last there were academic schools for girls such as Cheltenham Ladies' College, women had finally been allowed to qualify as doctors in 1876 and there were 212 of them by 1901 (and many became involved in the women's suffrage movement, particularly in Cheltenham), universities were opening to women and some even allowed them to be awarded degrees! The hated Contagious Diseases Acts, which subjected women to humiliating medical examinations and had been the subject of perhaps the fiercest campaign, were repealed in 1886.

Some gains were political – in 1869, single women ratepayers were given the right to vote in municipal elections. This was extended in 1894 to all women property-owners, and women could also become Poor Law Guardians and be elected to school boards. Women Poor Law Guardians were selected in both Cheltenham and Cirencester, making women's presence felt in the towns. These measures gave many women a taste of political participation and contributed to the argument that, if they were allowed to exercise this power, why could they not have the parliamentary vote? The response was often that women were able to experience the working of a town council, a local school or poor law supervision but could not gain experience or understanding of imperial or military matters, which many saw as the most important function of government. The fact that many men did not have this experience either was brushed aside, as was also the fact that many women whose fathers or husbands were in the army or colonial service *did* have some understanding, albeit at second hand.

It is clear that most of the above gains benefited middle- and upper-class women, and most of the women's suffrage proposals were to benefit the same groups. But this is not to detract from the urgency with which women who had tasted these relative freedoms sought further change – and Cheltenham in particular had many women of this kind. It was a town with many female heads of household, either wealthy in their own right or the widows of wealthy husbands. The presence of Cheltenham Ladies' College meant that there were also many educated women with ambitions for their pupils.

It is often not realised that only about 60 per cent of men had the right to vote in the early twentieth century. Those disqualified included men receiving poor relief, those who rented rooms below £10 a year, those who moved house often[1], men who lived with their parents, live-in servants and soldiers living in barracks. Most women's campaigns demanded equality with the existing male qualifications. The case for universal suffrage, the vote for all men and women, was much harder to present to an essentially conservative elite and even the newly formed Labour Party was divided on the issue

---

1   This disqualified many working-class households where movement even within small areas was common, either to find cheaper accommodation or, conversely, to move up the housing ladder a little.

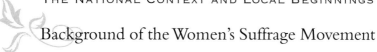

Background of the Women's Suffrage Movement

During the second half of the nineteenth century, the demand for women's suffrage was very much integrated into a movement demanding a number of reforms to improve the status of women. These included entry into the medical profession, higher education and the right of married women to own property. As has been seen above, much of this was achieved, but not without a determined and well-organised fight. However, many women argued that, with the vote, they could have influence on a wider range of issues that affected women and so it should be their priority.

From the 1860s, both a national framework and local societies were set up but there were a number of splits and splinter groups and the London bases found it hard to liaise with the regional groups and vice versa. The nature of their campaigning was focused primarily on achieving support of individual members of Parliament in order that a private member's bill might be successful. Petitions and debates with politicians were the order of the day.

Stroud, the 1866 petition and an outraged Queen!

The first significant petition was presented to Parliament in 1866 by the MP and philosopher John Stuart Mill. It contained 1,499 signatures (1,521 according to a parliamentary re-count!) of women from a wide range of backgrounds, collected via friends' networks. In the Cotswolds, there were thirty-one signatories from Stroud and its immediate area, a healthy number from such a small town, and one from Cirencester! There were none from Cheltenham, Gloucester or anywhere else in the county until one reaches Bristol. The sole representative from Cirencester was the Rev. Thomas O. Daubeny, who in the 1871 census was living at Perrotts Brook, with his wife, three children and three servants, and was Vicar of Poulton. One can imagine that one of the organisers or leading lights must have been a personal friend.

Analysis of the Stroud area signatories is interesting. Twenty-three of the thirty-one have been identified through the 1861 and 1871 census material. (Age given is that in 1866, when the petition was presented.)

Stroud signatories to 1866 Petition

Forename	Surname	Address	Marital Status	Age	Occupation
Elizabeth	BISHOP	Russell St., Stroud[2]	Wid	65	Registrar for servants
Adeline	BISHOP	Russell St., Stroud	Unm	37[3]	Milliner
Jane	BREWER	High Street, Stonehouse	M.	57	Wife of a blacksmith and farrier
Henry M.	BURGHOPE	The Croft, Stroud	Unm	22	Apprentice grocer
Mary L.	CLUTTERBUCK	The Cross, Stroud	Unm.	18	(scholar in 1861)
Ann	CLUTTERBUCK	The Cross, Stroud	M.	52	Wife of hairdresser[4]
Harriett	COLLINS	Quar House, Lower Lypiatt	M.	54	Wife of waterman
Sarah	EXELL	Union Building, Upper Lypiatt	M.	56	Wife of solicitor's clerk
Mary	EXELL	Union Building, Upper Lypiatt	Unm.	26	Schoolmistress
Mary (Millicent)	HORLICK	St. Mary's St., Painswick	Wid.	74	Retired from baking business
Elizabeth	HORLICK	St. Mary's St., Painswick	Unm.	34	Lodging house keeper
Sarah	HORLICK	St. Mary's St., Painswick	Unm.	34	Dressmaker
Rosa	HUMPHREYS	Roucroft, Upper Lypiatt	Unm.	36	Berlin wool dealer (a type of embroidery/ needlepoint)
N. Ann.	HUMPHREYS	Roucroft, Upper Lypiatt	Wid.	66	Berlin wool dealer
Mary	JACOB	Chapel House, Ebley	M.	48	Wife of Minister, Lady Huntingdon's Connection Chapel

---

2 In George Street in 1861. The Russell Street address is next door to the Clutterbucks – see below.

3 The 1861 census has her age incorrectly but her death records in 1872 corroborate the above. By 1871, she was married and living with her mother in Stroud.

4 In 1871, Mrs Clutterbuck was living off income from houses and interest from money.

Elizabeth	MONK	London Road, Stroud	Wid.	62	Dressmaker
Anne	MOUNTAIN	Russell St., Stroud	Unm.	50	Schoolmistress
Rosanna	MOUNTAIN	Russell St., Stroud	Unm.	44	Schoolmistress
Hester	POOLE	Chapel House, Ebley	Unm.	25	Berlin wool worker. Daughter of Mary Jacob – see above
Frederic	RUDGE	Acre St., Stroud	Unm.	26	Carpenter (lodger)
Harriett	RUEGG	Enfield Cottage, Stroud	M.	41	Wife of accountant and commission agent (she may have been helping in the business according to both 1861 and 1871 censuses)
Fanny	SLATTERIE	Ebley Villas, Ebley	Unm.	38	Governess – head of a small private school run at home
Annie	WEBB	Devonia Cottage, Ebley	M.	42	Schoolmistress – British School. Husband the Schoolmaster.[5]

What emerges seems to be a random collection of people with little in common in terms of occupational background, but occasional neighbourhood links! Did they have some religious affiliation in common? Children from families who attended the dissenting Lady Huntingdon's Connection Chapel run by Mrs Jacob's husband might well have been pupils at the British School where Mrs Webb taught, for example. However, it has been suggested that the signatures were collected through the efforts or influence of Lady Kate Amberley, who was then living at Rodborough Manor. She and her sister, Rosalind, the Countess of Carlisle, were fervent women's rights campaigners. Lady Amberley moved in a circle of women radicals (usually Liberal) including the first woman doctor, Elizabeth Garrett Anderson, who became her own doctor. Her campaigning, particularly a very famous speech in Stroud in 1870, earned her a biting attack from Queen Victoria.

---

5 British Schools were non-conformist in contrast to the National Schools which were Church of England schools.

The audience who came in 1870 to hear Lady Amberley deliver a lecture on the rights of women was more 'respectable' than 'cloth-capped' which perhaps explains why, according to her journal, there was hardly any applause and her speech seemed to 'fall very flat'. By that date, she had apparently managed to recruit only twelve members to form a local Suffrage Society.[6] Moreover, a woman addressing a public platform in 1870 was still highly controversial. Could a woman lecture and still remain a lady? Local landowner and JP, Sir John Dorington of Lypiatt Park, took the chair, lending the meeting respectability but, while her speech was accepted peacefully in Stroud, it caused an uproar elsewhere. The Letters page of *The Times* was buzzing with argument and counter-argument. But Queen Victoria's comments to Sir Theodore Martin, the official biographer of Prince Albert, were stinging. She wrote, 'The Queen is most anxious to enlist everyone who can speak or write or join in checking this mad, wicked folly of Women's Rights, with all its attendant horrors, on which her poor feeble sex is bent, forgetting every sense of womanly feeling and propriety. Lady Amberley ought to get a *good whipping*' (Sir Theodore Martin: *Queen Victoria As I Knew Her*, p.69). These comments were not revealed until forty years later, but the sentiments would have been shared at this date by many thousands of women.

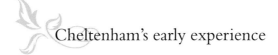

Cheltenham's early experience

The Cheltenham experience was typical of the national mixture of impetus and decline. A branch of the National Society for Women's Suffrage was set up in 1871, one of only twenty-one in the country. It is fascinating that the first branch secretary was Mrs Eliza Griffith, wife of the minister of Bayshill Unitarian Chapel, and a link with this chapel was maintained right up to 1914, albeit through two different ministers.[7] The treasurer was Mrs Eliza Robberds, the wife of another retired Unitarian minister. A similar early Unitarian link is seen in Cirencester through the person of Rev. Austin, minister of the chapel there.

Meetings were held but it is difficult to establish how frequent these were and how far they were initiated by local women, as the leading speakers were often national figures or from the larger and more forceful Bristol movement. Petitions were collected and presented, those of 1869 and 1871 being presented to Parliament

---

6   Presumably some of the twelve were signatories of the 1866 petition.
7   Rev. Joseph Hirst, minister of the chapel, addressed the society on 27 April 1879. The minister in the period 1900–14, Rev. Smith, was an even more prominent supporter.

by their Liberal MP Henry Samuelson, and a 'memorial' demanding equality for women ratepayers was drawn up in 1880 to be presented to Gladstone by a deputation from the town.

There is also evidence that local women were willing and able to speak on public platforms. Women speaking on the same public platform as men, so-called 'mixed speaking', was deemed shocking in this period. It appears that the Cheltenham Society was prepared to 'shock'. For example, in December 1880 Cheltenham Debating Society discussed the motion, 'Should women, equally with men, be invested with the parliamentary franchise?' Women were encouraged to participate in this debate and amongst these was Mrs Harriet McIlquham. In many ways, she was the most influential local figure in this period. She also embodies some of the main features and splits of the pre-1900 movement.

A Cheltenham pioneer: Harriet McIlquham

Harriet McIlquham appears in the late 1870s in Cheltenham as a supporter of the Women's Suffrage Society. She spoke at a meeting at the Corn Exchange in 1877 and, with her husband, appeared on a women's suffrage platform. James Henry McIlquham of Staverton House was surveyor to the Cheltenham Improvement Commissioners, and a well-known Cheltenham solicitor[8]. But in the late 1880s, Harriet was also a member of a more radical group, the Women's Franchise League, which campaigned not just on women's suffrage but on any issue which confined women to subjection, such as inequality in work and pay, education and access to local government. She became president in 1889 and through its National Council, she was in touch with many of the current and future leading lights of the movement, including the husband-and-wife team of Richard and Emmeline Pankhurst. She then helped to found the Women's Emancipation Union, which supported the rights of working-class women and explicitly the rights of married women over their own persons. The group had bitter battles with the Franchise League and nearly caused her to resign, so illustrating the ways in which the movement was fragmented by very slightly different emphases and often by personality clashes.

Until the 1890s, working-class women were not mobilised for women's suffrage,

---

8   They had lived in the High Street in the early stages of their marriage but moved to Staverton during the 1860s.

MRS. McILQUHAM,
Of Staverton House, Near Cheltenham. Died Jan. 24, 1910, Aged 72 years.

Mrs Harriet McIlquham of Staverton near Cheltenham, women's suffrage campaigner in the nineteenth and early twentieth centuries. A pioneer in local government, in 1881 she became the first married female Poor Law Guardian in the country. (*Cheltenham Chronicle and Gloucestershire Graphic,* 29 January 1910)

but then the Lancashire mill-women were galvanised into action in the Lancashire and Cheshire Women's Suffrage Society. Their 1901 and 1902 petitions of 67,000 women from the textile mills constituted a greater achievement than many others signed by women of middle- and upper-class backgrounds. The fact that Mrs McIlquham attached herself to groups which emphasised the rights of the working-class put her on the radical wing of the movement. This perhaps explains why she did not play a leading role in the Cheltenham Women's Suffrage Society, which seems to have petered out in the late 1880s, not to be revived until 1896. Her emphasis would not necessarily have been the same as the majority of campaigners in the town. Nevertheless, she managed to keep a foot in both militant and non-militant camps as the twentieth century progressed, attending local suffrage society meetings and giving some financial support to the militants. In 1907, she reluctantly conceded that patience had not brought results and that more militancy was perhaps necessary, but it was unlikely that, had she not died in 1910, she would have accepted the greater violence in WSPU tactics. She was happier in the Women's Freedom League (WFL) circles where militancy was more restrained.

However, Harriet McIlquham also represents another strand of nineteenth-century suffragism. She saw her role as partly to remove all the disadvantages that women faced in local government, not just as a precursor to the parliamentary vote but as a means to improve the lot of women. She was elected both as a Poor Law Guardian for Boddington in 1881, though as a married woman, she was not technically able to be so,[9] and also to Boddington and Staverton School

Advice for women candidates in local elections, Cheltenham branch of the National Union of Women Workers, 1904. This demonstrates the practical support needed for women to break into local politics. (Author's collection)

Women Candidates in Local Elections.

USEFUL HINTS.

How the Cheltenham Branch of the National Union of Women Workers procured the return of a Lady Guardian in one of the wards of the town, in 1904.

"At a meeting of the Executive Committee of the Cheltenham Branch of the National Union of Women Workers, it was resolved to work for the return of a Lady Guardian in a ward where a vacancy had occurred. The names of several ladies were suggested who seemed suitable and likely to be willing to stand.

It was further resolved to offer to pay legitimate expenses up to the sum of £5. The election to be run entirely on non-political grounds.

A Committee of three, besides the Hon. Secretary of the branch, was chosen to interview the suggested candidates. One being chosen, she and the Hon. Secretary procured the Burgess roll. Young lady volunteers were set to address envelopes to each voter in the ward with the candidate's Address. When ready, the ward was divided up into streets, and suitable ladies were asked to take so many streets, and to distribute the candidate's Address. They were to canvass as well as they could, but always on non-political lines.

The result was the return of the Lady Guardian.

It was a great help to have on the sub-committee a former Lady Guardian, as she was able to give help as to the details of election procedure."

Board. As the first married female Poor Law Guardian in the country, she was thus an important symbol of progress and was also able to look after the interests of women and poorer families. In the 1894 Local Government Act the rights she had claimed were enshrined in law for the first time, although other women followed only tentatively in her footsteps. Her attempt in 1889 to be elected as a county councillor for Central Ward, Cheltenham, to test whether women would be eligible as councillors, was unsuccessful but again she had shown what should or might

---

9   She was refused the right to vote in the election but her nomination was allowed to go forward! Married women were technically disqualified, but because she held property independently from her husband, she was allowed to remain in office when elected in spite of an objection to the Local Government Board. Hers was a challenge which blazed the trail for other women.

be possible. The rather modest leaflet (p. 33) from the Cheltenham Branch of the National Union of Women Workers indicates the guidance and confidence which women still needed to move into the arena of local government and civic life.

Move towards national unity and the emergence of militancy

But the disunity between different societies within the women's suffrage movement only hinted at what was to come. Most of the above groups campaigned to enfranchise about 1 million women at a time when the male electorate stood at about 7.9 million. It was not only that their focus was on middle- and upper-class women's rights, but that they did not even agree on whether the vote for married women of those classes was desirable. Mrs Millicent Fawcett, who was to head the non-militant movement in the crucial pre-war years, said that in 99 cases out of a 100 it would effectively give two votes to the husband, because 'Wives are bound by law to obey her husbands' (M. Pugh, *March of the Women*, p.24). A sorry confession from a convinced suffragist, and one which was attacked by other women!

In 1897, organisational unity appeared to have been achieved at last with the establishment of a democratic umbrella body, the National Union of Women's Suffrage Societies (NUWSS), under Mrs Millicent Fawcett. Some stability developed but frustration with conventional methods drove Mrs Emmeline Pankhurst and her daughters Christabel and Sylvia to set up a new more militant group in Manchester in 1903, the Women's Social and Political Union (WSPU), with the slogan 'Deeds Not Words'. Initially, its ties were with the infant Labour Party as the whole family were members of the Independent Labour Party (ILP). The WSPU became known as the suffragettes, a term coined by the *Daily Mail* to try to disparage their efforts as small and inconsequential. Thus the dual nature of the movement in the pre-war years was established, with the non-militant or constitutional suffragists in the National Union of Women's Suffrage Societies (NUWSS) facing the militant suffragettes in the Women's Social and Political Union (WSPU).

In 1905, the WSPU moved its headquarters from Manchester to London and the scene was set for much greater battles. 'Battles' is a word used advisedly, for the campaign was seen as a war and the use of military terminology was common. It was a war against an unsympathetic Liberal government, led by the apparently intransigent Herbert Asquith from 1908. Some WSPU women, Christabel

Pankhurst for example, came to see it as a more widespread war against men in general but many, as has already been seen, were supported by their husbands and did not see it in these terms.

Thus, the early-twentieth-century intensification of the struggle for women's suffrage began, a scene against which the women of the Cotswolds would play their part. How great a part?

Suffragists in Cheltenham: The Non-Militant Approach

As we have seen in Chapter 2, there had been some women's suffrage activity in Cheltenham in the second half of the nineteenth century, but it was not a major hub as Bristol and Birmingham were inevitably able to attract greater numbers and national interest. Harriet McIlquham had made her mark on the movement at national level. When she died, *The Common Cause*, the newspaper of the NUWSS (10/2/10), recorded her death thus:

> We record with regret the death, at five o'clock last Monday morning, of Mrs Harriet MacIlquham (sic), of Staverton, Gloucester. In her the cause loses not only a staunch local supporter, but one of the national pioneers, for Mrs MacIlquham in her early girlhood attended the first Women's Suffrage meeting ever held in this country. She was also one of the first women to sit on a Board of Guardians, and laboured zealously for many years in that office. Among her friends she numbered Mrs Wolstenholme Elmy, Mrs Pankhurst, Dr Louise Martindale, and many other early workers in the woman's cause. She also made a special study of historical women Suffragists, and wrote essays on them which appeared in the 'Westminster Review.' Mrs MacIlquham had but a short illness, and up to the last was working on behalf of Women's Suffrage, the Ethical movement, and other reforms.

As will be seen later, Mrs McIlquham's allegiance in the last few years of her life seems to have been to the militant Women's Freedom League rather than to the NUWSS, whose methods she felt were not making headway. It is the local WFL's floral tribute to her which shows the respect in which she was held:

A being breathing thoughtful breath,
The reason firm, the temperate will.
Endurance, foresight, thought and skill;
A perfect woman, nobly planned,
To warn, to comfort, and command. (*The Common Cause*, 29/01/10)

Mrs Swiney

There was another lady whose support spanned both the periods before and after 1900. She was Mrs Rosa Frances Swiney, wife of Major-General John Swiney. Mrs Swiney was born in Poona in 1847 when her father was an ensign in the 8th King's Regiment, and her husband was also born in Calcutta in 1832 to a military father. A colonial/military heritage was therefore engrained in them. By 1881, they were settled in Cheltenham in Atherington Villa, near Leamington Place, but their first four children had been born in India. Sometime in the 1880s, they moved to the twenty-roomed Sandford Lawn in Bath Road from where she conducted much of her campaigning and hosted suffrage events.

Rosa Swiney was instrumental in re-founding the Cheltenham Women's Suffrage Society (WSS) in 1896, and she dominated it and was revered as its president throughout its existence. As the wife of a military gentleman, both with a colonial

Mrs Rosa Swiney of the WSS speaking at the Clarence Street Lamp, the Cheltenham by-election, April 1911. (*Cheltenham Chronicle and Gloucestershire Graphic*, 29 April 1911)

heritage, one might expect her to be seeking voting rights for women of her class. This appears not to have been so. A number of her speeches, recorded in detail in the *Cheltenham Examiner*, referred to the position of the working-class woman. For example, in the Annual Meeting of early 1901 at the Chess Club Rooms, she addressed the company on the economic and industrial conditions of women workers, complaining that Cheltenham and well-to-do women were unaware of their problems. Restrictions on overtime in some jobs would harm women, whereas some jobs, such as charwoman, needed some restrictions in hours; a curious attack from the wife of a servant-employing household! Again, in 1906, Mrs Swiney regretted that there were no working-class women present and referred to the need for social reform as part of women's fight for greater recognition.

This kind of sentiment was echoed by Mrs Mary Stables in 1904 at a drawing-room meeting of the society at her home, 2 College Lawn. The hostess felt that the 'comfortable' classes of women should be more concerned about working women. She lived a very comfortable existence herself as the wealthy widow of a tea dealer, but she had spent some of their married life in the suburbs of Leeds. Perhaps some of the realities of the lives of the industrial working class had impinged on her while living there?

The membership: who joined the WSS?

This emphasis on rights for working women, although made alongside the demand for women's right to vote, seems at odds with the nature of the WSS membership at this stage and perhaps explains why their numbers were relatively low. If one examines who the supporters were in these early years of the twentieth century, it is clear that the platform and committee of the Cheltenham branch were dominated by women and men from the social elite. For example, at a meeting in the Victoria Rooms in April 1901, chaired by the MP James Agg-Gardner, there were three generals and two colonels on the platform, together with Mrs Swiney and her husband Major-General John Swiney, Councillor Hayward, and Mrs Swire (also born in India and living on her own means). The only injection of less privileged background was the presence of Mr Samuel Dix of Gratton Road who was a builders' merchant and also a local councillor. Amongst the apologies were those from another colonel, a major, and the heads and their wives of both Cheltenham College and Dean Close School.

A snapshot of these prominent supporters in early 1901 gives some idea of the nature of the local movement (all details taken from the 1901 census):

Prominent Cheltenham Supporters of the WSS in 1901

Name	Marital Status	Age	Occupation	Address	Comment
Eveline (Evelyn) CARGILL	S.	43	Doctor of Medicine	Lansdown Lodge, Lansdown Road	
Samuel DIX	M.	51	Builders' Merchant (employer)	Gratton Road	
John MACDONALD	Wid.	71	Retired Major General	31 Lansdown Crescent	
Richard ROGERS	M.	63	Dental Surgeon, Retired Colonel	Battledown Court	JP, candidate for South Ward, Cheltenham 1907
Rosa Frances SWINEY	M.	53		Sandford Lawn, Bath Road	
John SWINEY	M.	69	Retired Major General	Sandford Lawn, Bath Road	
Elaine SWIRE[1]	M.	39	Living on own means	Rodney House	
Cuthbert VICKERS	M.	63	Retired Colonel	5 Lansdown Terrace	
William WINSON	M.	70	Retired Major General	Cotswold Lodge, Pittville Circus Road	

---

1 Mrs Elaine Alice Swire was 'abandoned' by her husband Colonel Henry Swire in the early years of the century according to details from a divorce case of July 1914, when she brought a case against him for desertion. These details revealed that, when living in Berwick-on-Tweed in 1899, he told her that he expected to be posted abroad and that she and their daughter Yseulta (b. 1893 in Woolwich) should go to Cheltenham where Yseulta could be educated, and where his wife's friends lived. While he was fighting in the Boer War, he made her an allowance of £27 a month, but when he returned to England he refused to see them. Dr Grace Stewart Billings gave evidence in support of Mrs Swire's case. The home of Mrs Swire and her daughter in 1901 was rooms, perhaps only two, in Rodney House, Rodney Road. In 1911, her husband was similarly housed in Clevedon but either Mrs Swire had by then moved to Brussels, as the court case suggested, or was still in Cheltenham but evaded the census on principle. Elaine A. Swire appears as the author of at least three stories for London Society in the 1890s. One suspects a woman frustrated by her marriage and lack of freedom and opportunities, but one courageous enough to bring a divorce case, an action frowned upon for women.

APOLOGIES FROM:					
Francis ASHBURNER	Wid.	53	Retired Lieutenant Colonel	5 Lansdown Place	
William FLECKER	M.	41	Clergyman and Head of school	Dean Close Memorial School	
Sarah FLECKER	M.	40		Dean Close Memorial School	
Arthur GILBERT	M.	62	Retired Major	9 Cambray	
Ethel GRIFFITHS	M	26	Wife of surgeon	Cranford, Painswick Road	
John JOHNS	M.	35	Doctor of Medicine	3 Lansdown Place	
Lucie JOHNS	M.	38		3 Lansdown Place	
George PRUEN[2]	M.	49	Schoolmaster (Chelt College)	Leconfield (boarding house)	
Richard VASSAR-SMITH	M.	57	Railway and shipping agent	Charlton Park, Charlton Kings	Director of Lloyd's Bank, County Councillor for Charlton Kings
James WALKER	M?	60	Minister of Church of Scotland	Hilcot, Battledown	
Reginald WATERFIELD	M.	33	Schoolmaster Cheltenham College	Montpelier Lodge	
Mary WATERFIELD	M.	33		Montpelier Lodge	

It is somewhat surprising that there was such an emphasis on the rights of working women when other concerns may have been more relevant to the membership. The society needed support and it was the 'leisured' or professional classes who had the time and money to support suffrage campaigns.

Two other things emerge from the table. The age profile is skewed towards the upper end and the occupational background of the men is largely military or professional. However much the concerns of the working class were aired, the

---

2 It was his son who later became the partner in a solicitors' firm with Dr Earengey, the husband of the Cheltenham leader of the WFL. He himself died from drowning at Shrewsbury in 1908, an unexplained death.

impression given *to the public* of the nature of the Cheltenham WSS would have been of an elitist group.

Another discouragement to members may have been the personality of the first secretary, whose tenure lasted until 1902. Miss Emily Platt (b. 1867) was a forceful woman who was a teacher of English and Art and, by 1911, taught privately from home. Her father (who also taught English and Drawing plus Mathematics) had been Head of St John's School, but it is not known where Emily had taught. They lived at Roseville, Hewlett Road, until both her parents died after which she became a boarder, first in Cambray (1901) and later at 1 Glenfall Terrace (1911). She was a stalwart member of All Saints' Church and was praised in the pages of the *Echo* for her painting of the scenery for their church's production of *Beauty and the Beast* in 1901; it was apparently a simple design, not overblown like some amateurs tried to achieve. Clearly she was a woman of talent, devotion to causes and a background that might have enabled her to attract more lower-middle-class women, and men, into the society. However, her obituary in 1929 speaks of a woman with a difficult 'bluff mannerism' (sic) and 'somewhat dominating personality' (*Echo* 8/03/29). It is these nuances of character to which the historian is rarely given an insight – and, in this case, there can only be speculation about the damage she may have done to potential membership.

All the above factors suggest that it is not surprising that membership numbers struggled in the early years of the twentieth century. In 1900, it was reported that there were only 79 members, in 1901 there was regret expressed that they had so few members and that they had experienced a hard time ever since the society was formed, and membership fell to 53 in 1902. There was a small increase to 58 in 1903 and by 1906 it had risen to 114. It appears that the figures hovered around this number over the next few years. Theodora Mills, the secretary from 1902, suggested that 'with the notable exception of the late Mrs Harriet McIlquham, the founders were all members of the Primrose League' (*Echo* 13/02/18). It had been set up in the 1880s to widen the appeal of the Conservative Party and had admitted women in 1884 as they were invaluable assistants in canvassing and clerical work at elections. The Cheltenham WSS branch's close association with the Conservative Party may have limited its appeal, and Miss Mills suggested that membership numbers only rose because of an influx of Liberal women disillusioned with the government's attitude. When other suffrage societies were formed, there was some loss of members, but also some renewed interest in the whole movement.

It is difficult to be precise on membership numbers as the *Cheltenham Examiner* gave very full accounts until 1912 when, instead of reporting meetings, in a fairly even-handed manner, it asked for reports to be sent in from the secretaries of each of the four Cheltenham societies. This might have been a good idea at the time, but it is not so good for the historian: the content of the reports tended to be propaganda or news sent from headquarters.

Some early noteworthy figures in Cheltenham

Prominent in these early years was a professional woman, Dr Evelyn (Eveline) Cargill, who, with her partner, Dr Beatrice Harrison, ran a medical practice at Lansdown Lodge, Lansdown Road. Women doctors who had only gained the right to qualify as professionals in 1876 were prominent in the national women's suffrage movement. Not only did they feel that they deserved political as well as professional rights but they often had to, or chose to, tend to women and children whose rights seemed to be regarded as less important than those of the male head of the family.[3]

Dr Grace Stewart Billings was elected to the committee in 1903. She was Cheltenham's first woman doctor, establishing her practice at 3 Pittville Parade in 1899, accepting women patients only. At the time of her early women's suffrage activity, she was working from her marital home at Sussex Lodge near Pittville Gates. She had received a relatively progressive education, first at Clifton High School and then at Miss Bostock's Public Day School for Girls at 3 Bays Hill Villas. (It was a school for those whose commercial background did not allow them entry to Cheltenham Ladies' College.) Her father was a chemist who also ran the Co-operative Drug Stores in the High Street and she married the son of a prominent builder. Despite her distinctly middle-class background, she was in an excellent position to appreciate the hardships of both women and the lower classes when she was appointed one of two part-time medical inspectors of children in June 1908.[4] These women doctors may well have injected some harsh realism into the ideas of those with more privileged backgrounds and/or jobs.

Somewhat of a maverick in these early years, although a member of the committee in 1906, was Dr Charles Callaway, a widowed gentleman in his sixties living in Montpellier Villas. He had been a science lecturer in Wellington, Shropshire, when he described himself as an 'expert in Technical Education', and was a Fellow

---

3 The National Insurance Act emphasised this with sickness benefit being 10s for men and only 7s 6d for women.

4 The later section on Dr Burn v. Dr Garrett in Chapter 4 gives further insight into the school medical scene in Cheltenham and its association with women's suffrage.

Dr Grace Stewart Billings, first woman doctor in Cheltenham and woman's suffrage campaigner. She is shown here during the First World War with some of her nurses when she was part-time medical superintendent of St Martin's Hospital, Parabola Road. (By kind permission of the Billings family)

of the Royal Geological Society. Interestingly in the age of Darwin, he was trained as a Congregational minister but abandoned that, becoming an agnostic when his study of geology perhaps challenged what he had been taught. He frequently expressed his opinions at the reported meetings, talking of things such as men's hereditary selfishness and how the evolution of mankind included women as an important part. His most controversial statement at the annual meeting of 1903 was that the position of women was due to Semitic invaders! What would now be deemed politically incorrect seems to have gone unchallenged, presumably partly because he appeared to present the 'scientific' arguments which others could not. But the emerging study of eugenics, aiming to improve the human race through genetic selection, was very much on the fringe of much feminist thinking: Mrs Swiney explored it in some of her writings, for example, and joined the Eugenics Society, and some of Dr Callaway's ideas seemed allied to it.[5] The dangers of it being

16 Montpellier Villas, Cheltenham, the home of Dr Charles Callaway, WSS campaigner. He was also a scientist interested in eugenics and the Ethical Society. (© Paul Jones)

mishandled and linked to racism and rabid nationalism were not yet recognised.

Another area in which many women's suffrage followers were involved was the Ethical movement. Dr Callaway was President of the Cheltenham Society and in 1910 was lecturing on the topic 'Are We Better than Our Fathers?' while Mrs Swiney lectured on 'Ancient Wisdom and Modern Application' (*Looker-On* 01/10/10). The Secretary was Dr Earengey, also prominent in the WFL and WSS.[6]

Although there were undoubtedly hard and committed workers in the society in these early years of the century, there does not seem to have been much popular appeal or even much appeal to the many Cheltenham women of independent means and/or education. Those speeches which were reported were often full of

---

5   In her work *Our Indian Sisters* (1914), Mrs Swiney explored the way in which pure races in India had been defiled by the conquerors' sexual exploitation of women.

6   A spin-off from the society may have been a petition to the Gloucestershire Education Committee to teach science as well as religion. Signatories to this include fourteen identifiable women's suffragists, amongst them the McIlquhams, the Swineys and Dr Callaway.

dense literary and historical references which would not have drawn in the less educated groups: equally, the frequent references to the selfishness of the upper classes might not have appealed to those women whose better nature might have been cultivated.

Miss Theodora Mills (and her mother)

(Mary) Theodora Mills is a considerable figure in Cheltenham women's suffrage, not fiery but stubbornly persistent. She became honorary secretary in 1902 when she was just 28 and remained at the helm throughout the rest of its life. She later claimed that she and her widowed mother, Ruth, had long been supporters of the cause.

The prominence of Mrs and Miss Mills weakens the argument that, at this stage, the local society was dominated by military and ex-colonials. They were definitely 'trade', as Charles Mills had run a very successful wine merchant's business in the High Street (next to the Regent Hotel) in the last half of the nineteenth century and his widow and daughter were living off the proceeds. By 1902, they were comfortably settled in Lowmandale, Leckhampton Road. Ruth was his second wife and had been a teacher, living with her family in Carlton Place before her marriage. She had perhaps experienced the hardship of being a woman having to contribute to the family income without recognition of citizenship: it seems that her father had run a well-established silversmith and jeweller's business in Liverpool

Lowmandale, Leckhampton Road, Cheltenham, the home of Mrs Ruth and Miss Theodora Mills. Both mother and daughter were prominent suffragists, Miss Mills being the secretary of the WSS from 1902. (© Paul Jones)

Miss and Mrs Mills at the Mayor's Garden Party. (*Cheltenham Chronicle and Gloucestershire Graphic*, 2 August 1913)

but, when he lost that through either ill health or ill fortune, he stopped working and his wife and two daughters, Jane and Ruth, all began teaching, perhaps running a small 'dame' school.

Although it was her daughter who held office in the WSS, Mrs Mills often appeared on the platform at meetings in the early years of the century, and both appeared to contemplate supporting the WSPU by appearing at the first public meeting when it made a brief appearance in the town in 1906.

However, Theodora Mills made it clear in her annual report that, as the WSPU had caused some division of opinion, members should concentrate on the principle and also leave party politics behind (*Examiner* 19/12/06). She never endorsed their tactics but was not a sworn enemy. Indeed, five of her songs were published in a WSPU song sheet in 1907, including the one which later won an international competition. Set to the tune of 'Onward Christian Soldiers', it read (*Examiner* 22/07/09):

> Forward sister women!
> Onward ever more,
> Bondage is behind you,
> Freedom is before,
> Raise the standard boldly,
> In the morning sun;

'Gainst a great injustice,

See the fight begun!

Forward, forward sisters!

Onward ever more!

Bondage is behind you,

Freedom is before.[7]

It is difficult to gain an insight into Miss Mills' character although she appears so frequently in the press, in reports of the pre-1914 meetings and in her later letters about the movement. She appears calm and measured in her actions and statements, but then there are the occasional glimpses of forcefulness. She was not worried by public exposure at a time when many young women would have seen it as 'improper'. Both mother and daughter were among the eight named local women who claimed a parliamentary vote in 1909, thus challenging the law. Again, when representatives of all groups met the Liberal MP, Mr John Sears, in January 1907 to question him on his stance on women's suffrage, her more forceful side is seen. He had been an unexpected winner of the seat in 1906, defeating the local man, Agg-Gardner. The WSS was represented by six people but, in what appears to be a verbatim account of the exchanges, it was Mrs Swiney and Miss Mills who were most voluble (*Chronicle* 19/01/07). Indeed, Miss Mills had to be rebuked for interrupting Mr Sears and she made short sharp rebuttals of some of his statements.[8] However, the reports do not suggest she had the same powers of oratory as Mrs Swiney.[9]

Theodora Mills was prepared to take part in dramatic duologues about the women's cause, one called *The Lady and the Woman* which may have been written by her or another local woman as it is not in any collection of printed plays. The

---

7   The others were 'Song of the Suffragists' to the tune of 'Hiawatha', 'Rise Up Women' to the tune of 'John Brown', 'Women of England' to the tune of 'Men of Harlech' and 'In the Morning' to the tune of 'John Peel'.

8   He had expressed his support for women's suffrage in his election address but was not prepared to ballot for a bill to be put forward, so was seen as reneging on his position. It was as a result of his uncertain new stance that some women left the WLA as reported at the end of 1907.

9   Mrs Swiney's speech comparing the lack of civilisation and treatment of women in Britain with that in other countries is a masterpiece of scathing attack. She felt that only in Russia was there worse treatment and, even there, a widely-circulated cartoon poked fun at Englishmen's fear of women. Men in this country were losing the respect of their colonial 'Brothers' and their 'foes' on the Continent (*Chronicle* 14/12/07).

most successful propaganda play of the time, *How the Vote was Won*, was performed on a number of occasions, particularly in 1911, and Miss Mills was in the cast, alongside others who were trained 'elocutionists'. To add to these accomplishments, she sometimes sang or played the violin at WSS social occasions.

The lack of fear of public scrutiny is seen in Miss Mills' speaking at outdoor meetings, such as that at the Norwood Arms when she and Lilian How appeared under their red and white banner before a small but orderly audience[10] (*Examiner* 08/10/08). In contrast, an attempt to speak near Leckhampton Road polling station later in the year ended badly. Miss Mills was pulled off her chair three times by boys incited by a drunken man and the banner was seized by another. She was defended by three 'stalwart lady friends' who, sadly, are not named (*Examiner* 5/11/08). In 1909, she and her indefatigable mother, together with the even more indefatigable Mrs Swiney, went to Bishop's Cleeve and Gotherington to canvass and hold outdoor meetings with their 'second-best' red and white banner. Swindon Village was also tackled in spite of the rain, with Lilian How looking after their bicycles and the banner while Miss Mills spoke to a small group with children 'romping' around. Churchdown was a little more challenging in that it was difficult to gather an audience but, helped by drinkers in The Old Elm, about thirty-four listened to Miss Mills speak for an hour while Lilian How sold postcards: this time they were only disturbed by 'cackling geese' (reports from *The Common Cause*). Her biting report on a meeting at Leckhampton village again suggests that her anger could be roused and that the area was difficult to handle. She said that, as this was a suburb of Cheltenham, the inhabitants were 'lacking in the gentleness and courtesy of ordinary villagers, and rowdiness prevailed from the first word'. About thirty men assembled and urged a crowd of boys to howl and beat tin cans to drown her out. She and Miss How were also mobbed by the boys on their walk home (presumably to Lowmandale in Leckhampton Road).

It is also likely that Miss Mills was at the June 1908 London demonstration, as she issued appeals for women to go and march 'under our own banner' to Kensington and wrote of cheap rail fares and seats in brakes being available (*Examiner* 20/05/08). This was, we think, the 'new' banner with the coat of arms, which she eventually presented to the Cheltenham Museum and is now in the Wilson collection. She was also prepared to wave the Cheltenham banner, literally, in London demonstrations. She carried the Cheltenham banner at the huge 18 June 'Prison to Citizenship' procession and, in July 1910, she and another unnamed

---

10 Lilian How was sister of two notable women's suffrage figures – see Chapter 4.

One of Cheltenham's NUWSS banners, carried in at least one London procession. It can also be seen on p. 150. (© The Cheltenham Trust and Cheltenham Borough Council / Bridgeman Images)

member attended the NUWSS rally in support of the Conciliation Bill in Trafalgar Square. The secretary carried the old (red and white?) banner and the other held a petition banner in red, white and green (*CC* 21 July 1910).[11] It is surprising that she joined the first procession as it was a joint WSPU/WFL demonstration, but there was a truce which meant that militancy was in abeyance and so it might have been more acceptable to her. According to one report of 1910, all *five* banners were displayed, which suggests some excess! It does appear that she was very passionate about the visual representation and presence of the banners: an account she submitted to *The Common Cause* in 1913 emphasised how the platform at a meeting was decorated with 'several new banners' to replace those which had been destroyed by hooligans at the Pilgrimage (see Chapter 9). She even gives the detail of the wording on one – 'The Woman's Vote guards the Home' – which was to

---

11 This was relatively poor representation when 100 women represented Oxford.

counter the Antis' campaign of 'Man builds the Empire; Woman makes a Home' (*CC* 31/0/13).

The Conservative and Unionist Women's Franchise Association (CUWFA)

In late 1910, before the WSPU launched their major campaign in the town, the CUWFA established a branch. Its aims nationally were to counteract the anti-suffrage forces within the party which were in danger of putting the party out of step with the majority of the Liberal and Labour parties, as well as losing pro-suffrage members. They did not want a radical bill so felt that their MPs should be a force of moderation: after all, many men believed that those likely to be enfranchised first would be Conservative in their inclinations. Presumably, it was felt that the local Conservatives, with their pro-suffrage champion James Agg-Gardner, could not afford to lose the initiative to the WSS, although there was much co-operation in joint meetings. But as one of their councillors said: 'there was a strong strain in women and the extension of the franchise would be a great benefit to the party, though it was not for that reason he advocated it, but on the broad grounds of justice and the public welfare' (*Looker-On* April 1911). A quick attempt to lessen the self-serving appearance of his support!

The lady prepared to set up the branch and act as honorary secretary was Miss Flora Kelley. She was one of three sisters in their thirties living with their widowed mother in Ireton House in The Park.[12] All supported the women's cause but do not appear in the local press accounts before the CUWFA was formed. Flora Kelley was, however, associated with vegetarianism, so will have known the WFL figures associated with that movement such as Ruth Eamonson and Winifred Boult (see next chapter).

The CUWFA quickly gathered members, over ninety after three months in existence, perhaps partly due to the fact that registration was only 1*s* annually (*Looker-On* 12/11/10) and a plain badge cost only 1*d*. The branch seems to have stretched across the classes in a way that the others in the town did not.[13] It drew from the same class of ex-colonial and military families as the early WSS, with some

---

12 Her father had been in the army but had died in 1884.

13 Though it is difficult to tell because we seem to have a fuller picture of its membership than of other societies.

such as Colonel Rogers (retired dental surgeon) belonging to both.[14] These were people who were willing and able to host meetings in their large houses such as Mrs Currie of the sixteen-roomed 26 Lansdown Place, whose husband was retired from the Bengal Civil Service, and Mr and Mrs Bernard Geidt, of Bayshill House, recently returned from India, where he had been a civil servant. Miss Anne Welch, who took the major step of going to the House of Commons with Miss Kelley to lobby the MP for Tewkesbury, was the daughter of a naval captain; her mother and two sisters, all of Arle House, were members too. Colonel Fergusson of St Philips Lodge, Painswick Road, together with his two daughters, spoke publicly of his support for the cause as did Major Henry Brooke-Murray of Painswick Lawn, whose wife and two servants all signed the book presented to Agg-Gardner from which we can glean so much information.

But the CUWFA also drew some members who were not from the privileged elite but from the upper-working or lower-middle class. For example:

Mrs Charlotte Barton of Marle Hill Parade, wife of a town postman;
Miss Mary Channon of Oxford Passage, who was a hairdresser, living with her father, a painter and decorator;
Mrs Mary Edwards of Grosvenor Street, widow of a butcher;
Mr and Mrs Henry Granville of Upper Bath Road who were second-hand furniture dealers;
Mrs Sarah Houghton of Suffolk Road, a widow running a 'domestic agency';
Mrs Eva James of Great Norwood Street, a butcher/shopkeeper;
Miss Sara Vincent of Victoria Terrace, manageress of a dyers.

The main achievement of the association seems to have been the accumulation of supporters, both male and female, particularly after the election of James Agg-Gardner as MP in April 1911, as he had always been a supporter of the cause. They did hold some public meetings addressed by national speakers and it was reported that some went to the joint women's procession in London in June 1911, but co-operation with other local societies was more typical, such as a debate with the 'Antis'. Flora Kelley was also part of a joint women's deputation to Agg-Gardner in July 1911 to put the female point of view about the proposed Insurance Bill, which was to introduce a limited form of National Insurance. Each woman was to represent a section of women and, surprisingly in view of her background and

---

14 Drs Cargill and Harrison also belonged to both.

SUFFRAGE DEBATE.

TOWN HALL,
THURSDAY NEXT, March 6th, 8 p.m.

MISS HELEN FRASER,
Pro.

MRS. WENTWORTH STANLEY,
Against.

Chairman :
Alderman C. H. MARGRETT, J.P.

ADMISSION FREE BY TICKET ONLY

Advertisement for a women's suffrage debate at the Town Hall. (The *Cheltenham Looker-On*, 1 March 1913)

that of Mrs Geidt (see above) who accompanied her, Miss Kelley was to represent unemployed women. She pointed out that no trades covered by the bill included women.

Co-operation with the WSS was particularly marked in their efforts to convert the Conservative MP for Tewkesbury, Michael Hicks-Beach. After all, their own MP was already a champion of the cause. Cheltenham women, and some men, made a determined assault on Hicks-Beach, lobbying him at the House of Commons and at Sudeley Castle, while also holding meetings in Tewkesbury, Broadway and Winchcombe, often with Dr Earengey who led the Tewkesbury WSS.

The suffragist base in Cheltenham was therefore well-established, but it had to withstand an invasion by the more militant forces. Which group was to be more successful?

The Militants Arrive in Cheltenham

While the Women's Suffrage Society struggled to establish itself in Cheltenham, the impact of the formation of a more militant national organisation, the WSPU, was soon to be felt. But it was not at first clear whether Cheltenham would be able to sustain a militant group alongside the constitutional suffragists. Nor is there always a distinction between membership of the different societies: many women supported more than one, especially in the years before the escalation of WSPU tactics.

The WSPU appears in Cheltenham

The first public meeting of Cheltenham WSPU on 28 September 1906 was a big step forward but there was continuity with the past. Mrs Swiney, the president of the WSS, was to address the meeting. Earlier that year, she had written to the *Examiner* defending some of the tactics of the WSPU, such as asking questions at political meetings, and she denounced the 'discourteous behaviour' of the speakers who objected to this. In 1907, she expressed her anger that women in a civilised society could be imprisoned for demanding freedom and pointed out that university students often displayed hooliganism but this was tolerated (*Examiner* 11/12/07). At the first WSPU meeting, she returned to her theme of past years of hoping to see working-class women present and of the need for more social reform to improve their lot. By implication, she endorsed the WSPU approach as she criticised the ignorance and apathy of many people towards women's suffrage. But this did not lead to her defecting to the WSPU – she maintained her leadership of the WSS, while making some financial contribution to WSPU funds until 1908[1] and continuing to defend their right to act in ways which challenged the government.

---

1   WSPU First and Second Annual Reports.

Poster advertising Christabel Pankhurst's first meeting in Gloucestershire, 1907. The early WSPU ties with the Labour Party were soon broken. (Public display, Women's Library, London School of Economics)

Also at the first public meeting were Miss Theodora Mills and her mother Mrs Ruth Mills, both prominent members of the WSS, Theodora being honorary secretary since 1902. Mrs McIlquham was there too but showed her unease by saying that she could not endorse all the new methods employed by the WSPU. She appeared to revert to the older style of campaigning by asking all those present to take postcards to send to their MP. However, earlier that year, at a meeting in Gloucester at which Christabel Pankhurst was the main speaker, she had said that she was one of the 'old respectable workers' for the women's cause but that nothing would be achieved until they became 'outrageous'. She had gone along quietly in the movement for fifty years but now she was heart and soul with the 'insurgents' (*Citizen* 21/01/07).

The main speaker and chair in Cheltenham was Mrs Edith How Martyn. She described the origins of the WSPU in Mrs Pankhurst's contacts with the women workers in the cotton mills of the north-west. While this was not directly relevant to Cheltenham, she said that 'in a sense the homes of women were little factories' and the vote was needed to draw attention to the need of 'reform of taxation and for reform in the up-bringing and in the education of children'. Here she was concentrating on the social reform aspect of women being politically empowered, much as Mrs Swiney had done over the years. But she then pointed to the difference in tactics, with the WSPU attempting to get the ear of MPs by more forceful action and by making themselves felt at political meetings, by asking questions or interrupting the proceedings.

The How family

The women's suffrage movement in Cheltenham and its more militant aspect owes much to one family, the Hows of Cambray Place.

John How was a very successful grocer and tea dealer whose business, the London Supply Stores on the corner of High Street and Cambray Place, had been built up from lowly beginnings. He began his working life as a live-in grocer's assistant for a grocery business on the High Street, next to the Plough Inn. After he married Hannah Walker, formerly a domestic servant in Imperial Square, in 1872, he set up his own business on Bath Road, advertising the sale of good black tea at 2s per pound. He even applied for a drinks licence, in spite of being the son of a Baptist

The premises of John How's grocery business on the corner of Cambray and the High Street, Cheltenham. His two daughters, Edith and Florence, were key figures in the WFL. (Cheltenham Art Gallery and Museum's postcard in author's collection; image © Paul Jones)

104

North London Collegiate School for Girls,

SANDALL ROAD, CAMDEN ROAD, N.W.

3rd term - 1891

Fee for Registration of Application, Half-a-Crown.

APPLICATION FOR ADMISSION.

Christian Name, Surname, Age, and date of birth of the pupil, to be written in full.	*Edith How 16 August 4th 1890*
Profession or occupation of Father (if living) or Guardian.	*Tea Dealer*
Has the pupil been to school before? If so, where, and how long?	*The Hall Cheltenham 9 years Grosvenor College Bath 4 Terms*

SIGNATURE OF REFEREE.

(1.) To the Parent or Guardian of a pupil already in the School: or
(2.) To a Householder.

I recommend *Edith How*
for admission to the North London Collegiate School for Girls.

Signature in full *William Saunders.*

Address *Salopian Villa Winchcomb St Cheltenham*

I hereby agree that if my daughter be admitted to the School, I will abide by all the regulations, made or to be made, for the government of the School, or in regard to its Scholarships, Prizes, or other Endowments.

Signature in full of Father (if living) or Guardian *John How*

Date *June 11 1891*

Address *33 Cambray Place Cheltenham*

Edith How's admission form for North London Collegiate School. (By kind permission of NLCS Archive)

minister and in 1872 marrying at Salem Baptist Church! By 1881, the family was living at 33 Cambray Place and John was running the new business from there. There were six children, aged from 8 years to 9 months, four live-in grocery assistants and three servants.

It is the girls of the family who made a political impact, though they were supported by their parents.[2] Edith born 1874, Florence born 1877 and Lilian ('Lilla') born 1878 all became political activists. Where their ideas first arose is not clear. However, they were all educated from their teens at North London Collegiate School for Girls, a highly academic and enlightened school for girls, headed until

---

2   When Hannah How died in 1932, the obituary in the *Cheltenham Chronicle* told of one of the wreaths reading 'To a Suffragette Mother' (2/4/32).

her death in 1894 by Miss Frances Buss. She was a suffragist and, like her friend Miss Dorothea Beale of Cheltenham Ladies' College, a pioneer of girls' education.[3] The How girls could not be admitted to Cheltenham Ladies' College because their father was in 'trade'. They all went to The Hall School in Montpellier, Cheltenham, for their early education[4] and Edith had four terms at the less academic Grosvenor College for Ladies in Bath.

It is likely that many of their ideas were forged in London, and Edith acknowledged the influence of Miss Buss when writing in *The Vote* in 1910 (19 March):

> She knew how to develop a keen sense of self-reliance in them (the girls) … Then, too, we were made to feel that the privileges of higher education that we were enjoying had been won for us at great cost by other women and that we must value and use them accordingly. Miss Buss sometimes lectured to us on the lives of pioneer women, so that we naturally grew to reverence and respect those who had dared and suffered in pioneer work.

Edith How Martyn

Edith certainly took notice of Miss Buss's encouragement and exhortations. She was at the school for only two years from the age of 17 but, in that time, was a prize-winner and at the top of her form. She then gained an exhibition to Aberystwyth University College to study physics and mathematics, and in 1895 was awarded a scholarship to attend lectures and the laboratories of the Royal College of Science. She appeared to be ploughing an academic furrow but was not immune from the lure of marriage, and in 1899 she married George Martyn, then a science teacher. He was the son of Herbert H. Martyn who ran a Cheltenham business as successful as her father's.[5] Presumably Edith and George knew each other from

---

3   An anonymous poem, penned by one or more of their pupils, amusingly links the two:
    Miss Buss and Miss Beale
    Cupid's darts do not feel!
    How different from us
    Miss Beale and Miss Buss!

4   The Hall School was run by Mr Whittard with whom Florence's husband co-operated in passive resistance on paying rates for sectarian teaching in rate-supported schools.

5   H.H. Martyn's was the large decorative arts and ornamental ironwork business which was responsible for such prestigious work as fitting out ocean liners such as the *Titanic*.

their home town but their science connection (he is described as a physicist in the 1939 Register) may have brought them together in Aberystwyth or London. After their marriage, they lived for a short while in Naunton Park Road at a house called Liberty Nook (!), both working as science teachers.

At some stage, Edith joined the Independent Labour Party (formed 1893) and this radicalism led to her becoming one of the early members of the WSPU which had grown out of the Pankhursts' affiliation to the ILP. Her husband also came from a background which had taught him to have a social conscience: his father had established a mission for the poor in Lower High Street and a Working Men's College in Clarence Street, helped by teachers from both Cheltenham Ladies' College and Cheltenham College.

In 1906 she took the huge step of giving up a mathematics lectureship at the University of London to be joint full-time secretary of the WSPU. She was now in an influential position at the headquarters of the society: it was in this role that she came to Cheltenham to chair the first public meeting, described above, and to

VOTES FOR WOMEN.

As University Lecturer.   In H.M. Prison, Holloway.
Mrs. EDITH HOW MARTYN.
Hon. Sec. of the Women's Social and Political Union, 4, Clement's Inn, Strand, W.C.

Edith How Martyn, showing her both as an academic before her suffrage activism and as a prisoner while still in the WSPU. Publicity like this aimed to show the humiliation inflicted on 'respectable' women. (By kind permission of Kyla Borg)

support her sister Florence who was secretary. Just after the Cheltenham meeting, in October 1906, she was arrested when about 200 women were in the lobby of the House of Commons attempting to press their views on the Prime Minister, Campbell-Bannerman. She was one of ten women arrested outside in the street for trying to hold a meeting. The sentence of two months' imprisonment was harsh but reflected the views of a magistracy who just did not understand women coming into conflict with the police for the sake of a parliamentary vote. The government soon realised its mistake, after howls of outrage at the treatment of the women and the publicity that the cause gained, so they released the women after one month. Edith How Martyn can thus be classed as Cheltenham's first woman political prisoner!

Florence How Earengey

Florence How seems to have been less politically radical than her sister, Liberal rather than Labour in persuasion, but ultimately no less successful. Her career at North London Collegiate School was less illustrious: she matriculated in the Second Division whereas most of the pupils passed in the First Division. However, she went on to gain a University of London BA in 1898, possibly partly through private study. Like Edith, she also succumbed to the call of marriage to a young Cheltenham man, who had also gained a London BA in 1898, but First Class as opposed to Florence's Second Class! He was William Earengey, the son of a foreman click bootmaker[6] in his father-in-law's manufactory in the High Street. Although his parents were wealthy enough to employ one servant in 1881, this was not to last as his father died from TB in 1889. His background gave William a keen sense of social justice and of ambition. He had gained a place at Cheltenham Grammar School from the Highbury British School and, although this was not free, his education gave him a launch pad from which to raise himself.

Florence How and William Earengey married in 1899 in an unostentatious ceremony at Salem Baptist Chapel.[7] As William Earengey was an important part of the women's suffrage movement in his own right, as well as supporting his wife, understanding of what motivated him is useful and can partly be gleaned from this extract from his grandson's memories and perceptions of him:

---

6 A clicker was a skilled position as the man who cut out the leather and gave it to the workmen to complete.

7 The *Chronicle* 9/09/1899 reported that a number of the immediate friends of the couple were present at the wedding breakfast and that there were many 'handsome' presents, but the whole tone is of minimal fuss.

Florence How Earengey, head of Cheltenham's WFL throughout its existence. With her is her daughter Oenone. (*Cheltenham Chronicle and Gloucestershire Graphic*, 3 December 1910)

My grandfather was born at Cheltenham 10th January 1876; and was aged 13 when his father died. He could remember until his dying day the financial struggle his mother had in widowhood, to bring up her family: and of how uncomfortable he used to be in suits of clothing that did not fit. This background made him determined throughout his life to work and save, so as to provide financial stability and independence for his family.

He was educated at Cheltenham Grammar School; and was a classic example of the product of the old English Grammar Schools, which set out to provide the best of education to children no matter what their financial status. He was a classical scholar, keeping Latin and Greek texts on his bookshelves all his life: well read: and a generally cultured and cultivated man. He was a kindly man, who rarely showed any outward sign of anger. He had the ideal judicial temperament – wholly courteous, intelligent, and fair minded.

He always wanted to go in for the law, but could not afford the Bar until he had first made money. So he became a Solicitor, and joined the family firm of Steel & Broome in Cheltenham, where he was articled to his cousin Robert Steel [son of Edward Steel, an older brother of my grandfather's mother]. His Aunt Jane Steel funded him while he was in articles, by way of loan - which he repaid in full within a few years of qualifying. He was admitted a Solicitor on his 21st birthday.

Equally valuable is the analysis of Florence Earengey by her grandson – something of the character which propelled her into the women's rights campaign is revealed:

The first home of Dr William and Mrs Florence Earengey, 3 Wellington Square West, Cheltenham. Next door lived another elderly suffragist, Lucy March-Phillips. (© Paul Jones)

The How family was formidable – all well-educated and well-read, and great fighters of causes, great or small. Grandma was a suffragette. Her older sister, Edith, was imprisoned as a suffragette, and went on to become one of the first women to get an MSc from London University, and one of the first women Labour Candidates for Parliament. Grandma too was a graduate of London University … She had a more bubbling, electric personality than my grandfather, and was far more vociferous; but she shared his love of culture and of reason. Behind some of the How family there was a characteristic of hardness. Whilst Grandma Earengey could properly be described as a 'femme formidable', that hard quality rarely surfaced in her and she was a very loving grandmother. She dominated everything she did, by her magnetism and drive, but it was the quiet reason and ethics of Grandpa Earengey that was in the end the stronger influence on me.[8]

---

8   *Hope and Faith: A Family History*, Robin Stewart, 2013 Kindle edition.

Mr and Mrs Earengey started married life at 3 Wellington Square West, a very comfortable start which may have been facilitated by Florence's father, who had now moved to Torrington, Western Road,[9] from where he supervised the business while his son Ernest gradually took over. John How had invested in property over the years but it is not known whether the Wellington Square house was part of his portfolio. Living next door to them in Wellington Square was another suffragist from the older generation, Lucy March-Phil(l)ipps. Aged 82, she still attended the WSS 1903 annual meeting and there would undoubtedly have been conversations between the neighbours, if not exactly over the garden fence!

Lilian How

The third How daughter, Lilian, known as Lilla, is easily overlooked as she did not take any major role in the women's suffrage movement as her older sisters did. However, her name appears in various roles within the WSS and later the WFL, as literature secretary for example, and she was a steadfast supporter of Florence's leadership of the local WFL. Remaining at home with her parents and not having an education beyond North London Collegiate School, one gets the impression that she was living a more sheltered life than the other two – but many women like her rebelled precisely against this kind of restriction by joining the fight for women's suffrage.

The early WSPU in Cheltenham

After the initial interest surrounding the setting up of a branch in 1906, the activity seems to have died fairly quickly. Both Florence Earengey and Lilla How continued to be active in the local WSS and at the end of the year Mrs Earengey was elected to the committee. Whether this happened because she could not galvanise enough support for the newly formed WSPU, or whether her own support for the WSPU cause was only half-hearted, is not clear.

However, she did represent it in a women's suffrage deputation to the recently elected Liberal MP, Mr J.E. Sears, in early 1907. The composition of the deputation is interesting. The WSS was represented by Mrs Swiney, Miss Mills, Mrs Seaforth

---

9   John How had been born in Torrington, Devon. When Lilian How lived on her own in Albert Road after her parents' deaths, she also called that house 'Torrington.'

Mackenzie,[10] Mrs E. W. Wilkins,[11] Dr Charles Callaway (see Chapter 3) and Mr J. Nathaniel Hobbs, a member of the committee who was a retired Inspector of Inland Revenue and lived in Moorend Road. The WSPU was represented only by Mrs Earengey. Others present were there as support rather than as official representation. Three women were from the Women's Liberal Association but they said that they were simply there as individuals 'to listen'. Dr Earengey was there as a member of the Liberal Council. The Liberals were careful not to appear to be too hostile to their own MP. The President of the Women's Co-operative Guild, Mrs Lake, was in the deputation.[12] The WCG was a body which sought to bring together working-class women to give them a voice in the Labour movement and to press for social reform to benefit working families. In many parts of the country it was closely allied to the women's suffrage movement. Another woman observer was Miss E. Ursell 'representing working women' (*Chronicle* 19/01/07).

The deputation put two questions to the MP, asking him whether he would support a ballot for a women's suffrage measure to be introduced[13] and by what means this could be achieved. After eloquent pleas by Mrs Swiney, Dr Earengey and Dr Callaway, with interjections by Mrs Seaforth Mackenzie, Mr Sears stated his opposition to any bill which merely gave the vote to women on the same basis as men, i.e. one which would disadvantage working-class women. He objected to what he called 'class entrenchment'. They reached an impasse because the deputation had been arguing for a gradual enfranchisement.

Mr Sears then changed tack and began to condemn the attacks on the newly formed Liberal government, and particularly made reference to the disturbances caused by the WSPU. He argued that the 'scenes' had damaged the cause and the support of MPs. He described them as 'women who had got into the hands of the

---

10 Mrs Julia Seaforth Mackenzie was born in Northern Ireland and was the wife of a woollen merchant. They lived at 5 Montpellier Grove. She was a constant WSS worker in this period. Revealing her long history of support, she explained in the course of the deputation's debate with Mr Sears that twenty years ago she had collected 50,000 signatures for a petition from women workers in Belfast.

11 Mrs Emmeline Wilkins was the wife of a stockbroker and both appeared frequently at WSS meetings. They founded the Cheltenham Vegetarian Society and had lived in Queen's Road before apparently living semi-permanently in a vegetarian guest-house, of which more below.

12 Mrs Annie Lake was the wife of James, an upholsterer, and lived in All Saints Terrace. She was a woman in her fifties who had, since her one child had died, devoted many years of service to the WCG, as shown by a presentation to her when she resigned as president in 1908.

13 This was necessary if the government was not prepared to introduce a bill.

police and under the power of the law' and 'had immediately posed as martyrs'. He was undoubtedly referring to the demonstration of October 1906 when Edith How Martyn had been arrested, because Mrs Earengey quickly leapt to the defence of the women's behaviour and, by implication, her sister's. No agreement was reached at the meeting, but it seems to have been lively as one of the Liberal ladies expressed regret that there had been so many interruptions and that these had prevented her following his arguments as closely as she would have wished!

In this meeting, Mrs Earengey displayed in her defence of her sister some of the impulsiveness described by her grandson above, while Dr Earengey had the measured tone of his legal training. By this time, he was established in a solicitor's practice in Regent Street, having left Eldon Chambers in Clarence Street, had been awarded a Doctor of Law and was also about to fight for a town council seat for the Central Ward on behalf of the Liberals. He would not wish to alienate himself too far from the party he supported, nor to cast a shadow on his professional career.

The Women's Freedom League branch is formed

In late 1907 there was a dramatic split at the top of the WSPU, partly because of discontent with the autocratic rule of Mrs Pankhurst and her daughter Christabel, who did not want a formal constitution imposed on them. It was felt that Christabel in particular was 'cynical and cold at heart. She gave me the impression of fitful and impulsive ambition and of quite ruthless love of domination' (M. Pugh: *The March of the Women* p.178, quoting Helena Swanwick). However, the split was also about political opinion. The WSPU had its origins in the early Labour Party but it was again Christabel who seemed to be moving further to the right and away from its roots. The leading figures in the breakaway group were all loyal to the Labour Party and one of these was Edith How Martyn.

This small group, led by Charlotte Despard, joint secretary of the WSPU with Edith How Martyn, formed the Women's Freedom League (WFL) and initially took about 20 per cent of the WSPU membership away with them. Charlotte Despard was a distinctive presence,[14] who had lived and worked among the poor of Battersea in south London since the death of her husband, founding clubs for workmen

---

14 She was the sister of the future leader of the British Expeditionary Force in the First World War, Field Marshal Sir John French.

Mrs Charlotte Despard, who broke from the WSPU and became the president of the national WFL. A frequent speaker in Cheltenham, even after she was badly treated by the crowd at her first meeting at the Town Hall in 1908. (Wikipedia, George Grantham Bain collection at the US Library of Congress)

and boys and one of the first infant welfare centres with a nurse and care/toys for needy children. She became a vegetarian and a fervent Socialist and renamed her Despard Club 'Socialist Hall'. Also elected as a Poor Law Guardian, she set out to harry unscrupulous landlords and harsh Poor Law officials. She was therefore more than a theoretical campaigner and had earned great respect. 'She was born saintly' according to the Annie Kenney, a young suffragette close to the Pankhursts. Charlotte Despard came to believe that, without women's enfranchisement, 'The Utopia of noble citizenship, which has been the dream of my life, will never come to pass.'

The WFL described itself as militant but non-violent, 'constitutional militants': they were prepared to break the law, as we shall see, but not to attack property or people in any way.[15] This led to them being seen as a halfway house between the constitutional WSS and the militant WSPU, but they described themselves as suffragettes, not as suffragists.

---

15 Mrs Earengey reiterated this in a report to the *Examiner* in January 1912.

A noisy Cheltenham beginning

Edith How Martyn became the first honorary secretary of the WFL and was now in a powerful position to help her sister set up a branch in Cheltenham, which Florence seems to have been only too happy to do. The meeting of 6 March 1908 which introduced the WFL to Cheltenham was undoubtedly controversial. The speakers were to be Mrs Charlotte Despard and Mrs Teresa Billington-Greig. Mrs Billington-Greig was from a very different background. Forced to leave school at 13 to aid the family income, she began to learn millinery but hated it. She ran away from home to live with relatives in Manchester and trained as a pupil teacher before embarking on further study. While there, she formed an early association with the Pankhursts and the WSPU, being one of its earliest recruits. Mrs Pankhurst helped her to get a job in a Jewish school as, after a strict convent education, she had become an atheist and refused to teach religious instruction in a Manchester authority school. From that point she seemed to regard Emmeline as some kind of surrogate mother and it was a sense of personal marginalisation by the Pankhursts which was part of her motivation for the split with them in 1907. Like Edith How Martyn, she sacrificed academia when, in 1905, she became a full-time organiser for the ILP, and then from 1906 worked for the WSPU in London and in Scotland. It was here where she met and married Frederick Greig, who was the manager for a billiard table manufacturer; like many men, such as Edith How's husband, who were supportive of women's rights in this period, he agreed that on marriage their surnames should be joined.

There had been great publicity for the Cheltenham Town Hall meeting at which these two very different ladies were to speak, with large posters and the ever more popular 'chalking of pavements'. The disdain with which one reporter for the *Examiner* (11/03/08) described 'the undignified spectacle of a young woman flopping down upon her knees to chalk advertisements of the meeting on a pavement in the Leckhampton district' displays the way in which women were perceived to be flouting social propriety.

The problem with the meeting seems to have been its very popularity! In a letter of 1918 (*Echo* 13/2/18), the former secretary of the WSS, Theodora Mills, recalled it as the most crowded meeting of the local movement, perhaps reaching as many as 1,000 attending. The organisers had only booked the Supper Room, not the main hall, and half an hour before the meeting was due to begin there was already an overflow from the 620 seats allegedly put out. People overflowed into the adjoining refreshment room and the corridor, and some of the crowd spilled out onto the street. Unfortunately, this was an explosive situation as many of the crowd were opponents, not sympathisers, and the ensuing events allowed press critics to have a field day. For example, a journalist for the *Examiner*, who had not been assigned to report the meeting but went along out of 'curiosity', was moved to write a thoroughly caustic account of the whole meeting and of his experience of being ejected from the corridor by the police. He made it sound totally out of control, a version disputed in a subsequent letter to the paper from Dr Earengey who described the meeting as 'quite orderly' in the Supper Room in contrast to the rowdiness of the corridor. He did, however, blame himself for not having secured enough stewards and for not alerting the police until the afternoon of the meeting (18/3/08).

So what happened at the meeting to cause such headlines as 'Rowdy Meeting' (*Looker-On* 7/3/08) and 'Disturbance in the Corridor' (*Echo* 7/03/08)? Mrs Earengey chaired the meeting, as Mrs McIlquham, although present, felt unwell. Apart from the main speakers, there were on the platform Mr Malcolm Mitchell, the national secretary of the Men's League for Women's Suffrage, the 'doughtiest of champions of the theory of feminine superiority' Mrs Swiney, Miss Theodora Mills secretary of the WSS, Dr Grace Stewart Billings, Mr McIlquham, husband of Harriet, and Mrs Wilkins. Mrs Despard remarked that much had happened since, little more than a year ago, she had appeared on a Cheltenham platform.

Cheltenham Town Hall, *c.*1905. The scene of many women's suffrage meetings, some peaceful and some not! (Postcard, author's collection)

She described with great vivacity how the movement had been invigorated by the 'spark' of the more militant tactics and how arrests and imprisonment were not going to stamp out the agitation. The agitation was growing and growing and it was no use to shut their eyes to it. At some length, she argued that it was economic subjection of women that necessitated their right to vote so that they could become equal partners in the home. Women would then be able to press for domestic and workplace reforms and for more educational opportunities. She reminded her audience that 'woman was the mother of the coming race, and the man as well as the woman depended on what the mother was and what she had trained to be'. But she also emphasised how brute force (male?) would not always rule – that 'we were moving towards that which was greater and higher mentally and spiritually'. In a passage which must have been delivered with a passion and eloquence which was very moving, she said:

> what they were asking for was a key to a life that was better for the women for the little children, and for the whole community. It was because they had the knowledge of sorrow, because they were citizens of society as it now is; it was because of the cries of the hungry children, the sweated workers, and the misery of the one-roomed dwelling of the poor; it was because of all these things that they were working, to help to put these crooked things straight; and she was thankful and proud to say that they had some of the finest men of the day with them.

However eloquent Mrs Despard was, according to the *Echo* reporter, Mrs Billington-Greig's speech was 'an oratorical feat of a high description'. She emphasised the 'elementary justice' of giving women the right to vote when they had to pay taxes and observe the laws made by Parliament. She made stinging attacks on the way the 'male' parliamentary system operated and, to laughter and applause, cast doubt on the intelligence of men. Unless the women made 'a howling row' they were never listened to and it was for that reason that the women had to persist. 'Only the strong, eloquent and noisy could hope to get the ear of the House of Commons.' This meeting was relatively well-received apart from someone tooting a penny squeaker, whom Mrs Despard soon quietened with a disparaging remark, but the overflow meeting was more difficult. Dr Earengey presided and called upon Mrs Billington-Greig but she was interrupted by youths in the corridor singing 'Put me among the girls' among other ditties. When Mrs Despard stood up to speak, the men and youths refused to listen and threw insulting remarks at her. She gave up and announced that in no town in England had she met with 'such a senseless or disorderly crowd' before leaving the hall in disgust. This was some condemnation as Mrs Despard had family ties with Cheltenham.[16]

Finally, the police arrived at the Town Hall and removed the disorderly elements, and Dr Earengey said he was ashamed of Cheltenham. A letter to the *Examiner* (18/03/08) from Mrs Ida Roberts[17] enlarged on the rough behaviour, refusing to let ladies leave when they wished and 'one Hooligan called out to Mrs Despard a remark so offensive and so indecent that it is impossible to repeat it.'

A slightly different perspective was taken by the *Examiner* reporter, who was there out of interest. Apart from criticising the lack of organisation and forethought, he was scathing in his assessment of Mrs Billington-Greig's contribution to the mayhem:

> Mrs Billington-Greig may be very clever – though to write her pamphlets and make her speeches does not necessitate any high order of genius – and she would be cleverer still as an advocate of her principles if she would avoid raspishness. She it was who gave that overflow meeting away … Sometimes the opposition bursts out suddenly spontaneously, like the ignition of some highly inflammable material. But more often the spark is fanned into flame by the tactlessness of the platform … Mrs Billington-Greig sniffed the battle like a war-horse. References to our masculine prejudice, to our ignorance, to our ridiculous assumptions of superiority, etc., etc., were pointedly made to the Corridor. And the Corridor felt that its chance had arrived. (11/03/08)

He regretted that, as a consequence, Mrs Despard, 'of the haughty mien and grey hair and flashing eye', was not treated with respect and does imply that his fellow men in the Corridor 'behaved ourselves (sic) execrably'. But he continued his attack on Mrs Billington-Greig and her 'pitiless flow' which continued in the Supper Room.

Opinion was therefore divided, and tensions had been raised more than at any point in the history of the women's suffrage movement in Cheltenham. The level of

---

16 Her brother-in-law, Rev. George Despard, had been vicar of St Luke's and had lived next door to the Swineys. After his retirement through ill-health and death in 1903, his widow and daughters lived at Undercliff, Leckhampton, so Mrs Despard had nieces in the town. The relationship was perhaps not strong as there is no mention anywhere in her speeches of the family link.

17 Mrs Ida Roberts of Elmstone Vicarage was the 60-year-old wife of the vicar, living in comfort in fifteen rooms with two servants.

opposition at the meeting was partly caused by the national attention that the arrests and imprisonment of the suffragettes had aroused. The WFL had gained notoriety from the attempt by four women to get through the barriers to the king's coach when he was en route to the opening of Parliament. This was to present a petition to the king, but the perceived impropriety had aroused attention. Edith How Martyn nearly made more of an impact at the opening of Parliament. Fellow Socialist, the MP Philip Snowden, wrote to offer her a ticket to view the royal procession from the gallery leading to the House of Lords, a position from which she could have stepped forward to present a petition:

Saturday 25th January '08

Dear Mrs Martyn

I am sending you a ticket of admission to the Royal Gallery of the House of Lords. It will admit one person, who will have no difficulty in handing her petition to the King. All I ask is that you will say to the Press, if they ask how you got the ticket, that it was given by a friendly MP. Mention no name.

I would suggest that you choose to do this thing, some woman of gentle and refined appearance as well as intrepidity of spirit as such would receive more favour in the eyes of His Majesty. Why not your sweet self?

With kindest greetings,

P.S.

(R. Fulford: p.173)

It seems that either she did not take up the offer, or that her effort was forestalled by the Lords officials having to deal with the removal of a rather 'bizarre' gentleman who claimed to be a peer! An opportunity missed!

Lessons learned?

Attempting to learn lessons from the adverse publicity which the overcrowded meeting attracted, the WFL hired the large hall in the Town Hall for a meeting on 4 July 1908, again to be addressed by Mrs Despard and Mrs Billington-Greig. Edith How Martyn chaired the meeting and introduced some of the members of the National Executive who had been holding a meeting in Cheltenham that day, perhaps persuaded by her that the town would welcome them? However, there were rival attractions that evening as a summer pageant was being held, one of many organised around the country by Mr Louis Parker – at least, that was Mrs How-

Martyn's excuse for the fact that the hall was barely a quarter full, with perhaps only a hundred present. It may have been the case, however, that all but the keenest had been put off attending by the scenes which had accompanied the meeting in March. But the fact that even the obstructive hobble-de-hoys from March were absent perhaps suggests that interest had waned.

Both Mrs How-Martyn and Mrs Despard addressed the issue of the justification of militancy. The former said that they had been forced to take up that stance and Mrs Despard and Mrs Billington-Greig both argued that militant methods were not only justified by the injustice of women's position but by their success.

Although this meeting went ahead without the commotion of the earlier one, there was some controversy surrounding it. Mrs Emma Sproson, a WFL campaigner from Wolverhampton and the only working-class woman on the National Executive Committee, was summoned to court for chalking the pavement to advertise the meeting. While on duty in the Colonnade, at the north end of the Promenade, PC Robert Howe challenged the defendant who answered, 'You cannot stop me'. When charged in court under a bye-law of 1900, Mrs Sproson answered that: 'this Court is established on laws made by the will of men, and in which women have no consent. Therefore, I don't consider the Court is a proper authority to try me. I refuse to make any promise, pay any fine, or enter into any recognisance' (*Examiner* 09/07/08). She was told that the fine would be 5*s* or seven days' imprisonment. A number of women's suffrage campaigners were in court to support her; when they applauded her defiant stand, the chairman threatened to clear the court. However, he did ask Mrs Swiney if she wanted to ask a question and, perhaps recalling what had happened to Mrs Despard in March, she asked whether there was any bye-law 'respecting the use of foul, obscene and indecent language'. The chairman ruled that this question was not connected with the case. A point had been made publicly, however, and the fact that the fine was paid by someone in court suggests that some in Cheltenham supported this kind of action. It should be said that 'chalking' was a common method used to advertise meetings but, where bye-laws did not exist, women could not be charged as Mrs Sproson had been. Nor, according to a letter of Mrs Swiney, were similar acts prosecuted in Cheltenham. She wrote that, 'I have myself seen the pavements of this town, especially on the Bath road, chalked with notices of Salvation Army meetings, of notice of demonstrations on Leckhampton Hill etc., but I have never in the police reports read of any summons being served on an Salvationist or demonstrator for "right of way"' (*Echo* 4/7/08).

Another incident only reported via a letter to the *Echo* of 3 July also concerned the presence of Emma Sproson. Sardonically headed 'The Superiority of the Male', it alluded to an outdoor meeting which she had addressed from a chair and had

A typical anti-suffrage postcard showing that women should remain in the home and were neglecting their family duties. (Author's collection)

been heckled and booed with the words, 'Why don't you go 'ome and mind the kids?' He concluded that there was 'absolutely no comparison between the female and the male at these meetings: the one using nothing but logic and fact – who wants these in politics? – the other employing the splendid and ever-cogent weapon of force, bulk and magnificent animal strength'. This observer was dismissive of male tactics though his heavy sarcasm may have eluded some readers. Another letter in the same column decried suffragette tactics against the background of stones having been thrown at the windows of the prime minister's house. But Miss Ruth Eamonson (see below) suggested that the force of the mob was such that there was danger of the speakers being thrown from their chairs, and that they were threatened by 'stupid inarticulate booing and shouting from the enlightened citizens of this great educational centre' (*Echo* 4/7/08).

More violence

The theme of aggression towards Cheltenham suffragettes of the WFL continued. Even *The Times* reported the letter sent to the *Examiner* (03/09/08) in which a Russian journalist, Zenoide Mirovitch, described with horror the scene she witnessed in Cheltenham on what she claimed to be her ninth visit to England. Cheltenham was honoured by the presence of this remarkably brave woman who had campaigned for women's rights in Tsarist Russia, and had become a journalist in 1897 to escape censoring of her theatre work. She lived in England for periods but was also well known on international suffrage platforms (*CC* 15/04/09). The writer describes a meeting of six or seven ladies of the WFL assembling for a meeting at the crossroads at the foot of Leckhampton Road, one of whom was Edith How Martyn. (It is likely that there were other local members involved.) The women were stopped from speaking by 'hooligans' yelling, singing and pelting them with rice, dirty paper and other things.

What she found more appalling than this behaviour of 'the scum of the population' was the fact that 'decent-looking' men allowed this to happen. Only one man attacked the youths and a fight then broke out. To add to Ms Mirovitch's disgust, a policeman looked on without intervening[18] and then told the women that they were obstructing the way, which was against the law. The women moved to the other side of the road, near the corner with Langdon Road, where they managed to conduct a quiet meeting, although the writer was hit by a plum at the end of it, apparently because she had told the 'hooligans' what she thought of them! This was something she did not expect from England when she was used to being treated with respect in a far less liberal Russia. Again, Cheltenham does not emerge from this story with credit.

This is even more evident when one realises from a different report that it was a joint meeting with the suffragists of the WSS with Mrs Swiney and Miss Mills in their number – but, as stated before, the distinction between the suffragists and suffragettes was not recognised by many people. And many of the women did not recognise these clear distinctions either. The fact that they were prepared to appear on each other's platforms or give other support is evidence of this. An example occurred in October 1908 when the WFL held a Town Hall meeting to hear Mrs Despard. Although WFL Florence Earengey chaired the meeting and her husband and sister Lilian ('Lilla' – now the literature secretary) were present to support, Dr Callaway and Miss Mills from the WSS were on the platform, along with Miss Mills' mother, Mrs Ruth Mills. Miss Lilian Faithfull, Principal of the Ladies' College, was also present (*Echo* 05/10/08).

The meeting also illustrated the growing violence that the women were attracting. Mrs Despard sported a scar on her forehead which gave her the opportunity to

---

18 The *Echo* report says he did intervene.

describe how she had acquired it. In May, the national WFL pioneered the delightful propaganda method of caravanning, a method copied by the WSS! In doing this, they were able to reach villages otherwise cut off from political life, but they also received publicity. In her second spell with the caravan as it meandered through Kent, Mrs Despard was hit by a stone as she attempted to address a crowd in Maidstone. The van was brought to the square to try to give her and the other speaker some refuge from the hail of stones but some of the crowd attacked the van, breaking its windows and the tail-board. She made two points about the incident. She felt that there was some organisation of the opposition, and she compared the sentence handed out to women who broke windows of Asquith's house with the fact that no report was received by the police of the riot and 'of the injury done to them and their property' in Maidstone. If the law was not protecting her, and women like her, why should they pay taxes?

Indeed, tax resistance was a method which the WFL national executive urged on its members in 1909. The slogan 'No Vote, No Tax' was widely spread. When middle- and upper-class women resisters refused to pay their taxes, their household and personal goods were seized and put up for auction: this gave the cause excellent publicity. Very often the goods were bought by wealthy sympathisers and returned to their owners. When the Women's Tax Resistance League was formed in later 1909, however, it was independent of the WFL, although women such as Edith How Martyn were supporters. I cannot find any instances of this resistance being adopted in Cheltenham or any town nearby. One meeting is recorded in October 1911 but the local speaker was Mrs Swiney, not a WFL crusader, who gave her support as an individual rather than as a leader of the WSS. This is perhaps surprising as the Earengeys were involved in the non-conformist campaign not to pay rates to support Anglican schools, and Dr Earengey defended individuals caught up in the campaign. Of course, this was a different cause, but the same principle was involved. Yet the Earengeys did not venture into tax resistance.

CHELTENHAM WOMEN FIGHT FOR THE VOTE AND OTHER 'CAUSES'

Cheltenham's first woman prisoner

Although Cheltenham-born Edith How Martyn had been imprisoned in 1906 when a member of the WSPU, she was not resident in Cheltenham by then. Technically, therefore, the first Cheltenham prisoner for the women's cause was Madame Lilian Borovikovski(y). In 1909, she was 27 years old, married to Sergei Borovikovsky who, according to the marriage report in the *Echo* of June 1902, was working in the Finance Ministry in St Petersburg. He was also later described as a 'senator' of the 'old regime'. How she met her Russian husband must remain open to speculation: similarly, why was she not in Russia when the *Echo* said that after the wedding they were going to leave by boat for Russia, their new home? (There is a reference of her having returned to Cheltenham from Russia in 1911, so she did perhaps visit her husband occasionally, and they did have a son Sergei in 1904.) No more references to him have yet been discovered, apart from the fact that she was described as a 'widow' when she died in 1926, a sad death in Gloucester Mental Hospital at the age of 45 or 46. If he was attached to the 'old regime', could he have perished during the Bolshevik Revolution?

Lilian Borovikovsky's earlier life has some mystery attached to it too. She was born in Birmingham in 1880 to Louisa and her 'partner' Christopher Prust, who was a vaccination officer. They were recorded as married in the census of 1881, with daughter Emily aged 2 and Lilian aged 7 months. But the marriage of Louisa and Christopher took place in 1882! Her mother's origins are uncertain, but her obituary suggested someone with a keen mind, who could also play the cello. According to her obituary, Christopher Prust died in the late 1880s, but no record of his death can be found. Yet Louisa went to Cheltenham with her two daughters to live with her mother-in-law at Jersey Place, Hewlett Road. By the 1901 census, Lilian is not with her mother and younger sister and cannot be traced elsewhere. Did she go to Russia – did she then meet her future husband? At some stage she must have been at Cheltenham Ladies' College as she is named among the Ladies Guild in one year.[1]

This tantalising mystery remains, but her action and the consequence in February 1909 are not in doubt. We have the accounts from *The Times* and a report of Mme Borovikovsky's speech to the Cheltenham WFL on her return from prison. *The Times* (19/02/09) suggests that, after a meeting at their offices in the Adelphi, Mrs Despard and others decided to go to the House of Commons to make another attempt to present a petition to Prime Minister Asquith. (An attempt to get to Downing Street the previous day had resulted in the arrest of twenty-four women.) This called upon the government to enfranchise women in the current session of Parliament, and declared that 'the continued denial of political liberty to women' was a direct incentive to use unconstitutional methods. Mme Borovikovsky said that she had volunteered to take the branch's resolution to the prime minister, and that 'next time she hoped to be accompanied by many others from Cheltenham'.

The arrest of eight people including Mme Borovikovsky and one man, the socialist author Joseph Clayton, occurred at the entrance to the Commons. When about twenty or thirty women arrived at the House, walking in twos and threes, they found a double barrier of police ranged against them and constables guarding other entrances. Mrs Despard told the chief inspector that she wished to take a resolution to Mr Asquith, but she was told that she could not do so but that he would pass it on. Mrs Despard refused to do that or to go away and she and two others were arrested. Then a number of others tried to force their way through but were kept back by the police, who then arrested them. This incident was described

---

1   Her mother is similarly mysterious, not only in her first marriage, but in the age she recorded in the censuses. It was not unusual to mask one's age, but in 1891 she declared 37 when she was 41, in 1901 45 when she was 51, and in 1911 48 when she was 61! The latter may have been because she married the younger Charles Teague who was only 43 in 1911, but when she died it was remarked upon that she looked much younger than her nearly 80 years. This is only worth dwelling upon because Lilian's mother may have been living a life built upon lies and Lilian's own fragility, revealed at the end of her life, may have been a direct result of this – coupled with a somewhat unusual marriage. Lilian's older sister, Emily, also embarked on an unusual marriage to Dr Derossi, from St Petersburg, and she was living in Finland when her mother died in 1929.

The Holloway brooch, presented to WFL women like Cheltenham's Mme Borovikovsky, on their release from prison. (Ebay advertisement)

as an attempt to 'raid' the House of Commons! The women were taken to Cannon Row police station and Mme Borovikovsky was charged with obstructing the police. As she said, this was ridiculous when there was such a large number of police present, some mounted. Some of the defendants were bound over on undertaking not to breach the peace, but Mme Borovikovsky declined to be bound over and was ordered to pay two sureties of £10 each or undergo one month's imprisonment. She recounts that 'owing to the state of her health', she was compelled to leave Holloway after nearly a fortnight but she did not state that this was because she went on hunger strike so it must have been for other reasons (*Echo* 24/03/09).

Cheltenham WFL was very supportive of Lilian Borovikovsky's action. Mrs Earengey welcomed her back and expressed the branch's deep gratitude for her 'self-sacrificing devotion to the cause'. She felt that there was nothing violent about the methods used and that the word 'raid' was inappropriate. Two books were presented to Mme Borovikovsky – Mrs Swiney's *The Awakening of Women* and Mrs Perkins-Gillman's *Women and Economics*, tied with the colours of the WFL. The Holloway brooch, which the WFL first used to honour its prisoners at the end of 1908, was presented to her and it was announced that the branch would be contributing to the Despard prisoners' fund.[2] Mme Borovikovsky was thus the proud owner of the symbol of imprisonment – one wonders how much she wore it among polite Cheltenham society!

---

2   The WSPU copied the idea for its prisoners in 1909.

The campaign continues in Cheltenham

The WFL continued its campaigning in Cheltenham with regular meetings. The Earengeys' Liberal connections may have been the reason why they welcomed to their meeting, at the end of March 1909, Countess Russell. She was a colourful character who had, as she put it, broken from the Liberal Party of which her husband's grandfather, Lord John Russell, had been such a proud part, because of the government's refusal to introduce a women's suffrage bill. The Supper Room of the Town Hall was well attended and the noteworthies of the local movement were on the platform – Mrs Swiney, Mr and Mrs McIlquham, and Mr James Ransford, a retired sub postmaster from Leckhampton.

As Marion (Mollie), Countess Russell's marriage to Frank Russell caused him to be tried for bigamy in 1901, there was a whiff of scandal surrounding this 'fat, florid Irishwoman, with black curls, friendly manners and emotional opinions'. She was also related by marriage to Lady Amberley, the woman who had been so heavily criticised by Queen Victoria for her speech in Stroud in 1870. However, she was heard with courtesy as she told the audience how she hated public speaking and 'it was an awful bore living in hotels' but that she was prepared to put up with discomfort for the sake of the cause (01/04/09). Living in hotels was hardly on a par with imprisonment in Holloway! It is significant that Mrs McIlquham was prepared to chair the meeting when she retained some doubts about the nature of militancy; but she defended the women from the charge of being 'hysterical females'.

The composition of the WFL committee in 1909 reveals the overlap with the WSS – both Miss Theodora Mills and her mother were on the committee, as of course were Florence Earengey and her sister Lilla How. Officials of each were therefore members of the other group. Such 'official' overlap was less usual than at grass-roots level.

An alternative lifestyle

One of the landmark efforts of 1909 was the unsuccessful attempt by eight local women to register their names for parliamentary votes. This was a joint attempt with the WSS and the WFL representative was Miss Ruth Eamonson (with Miss and Mrs Mills also on the list). She was a woman in her mid-thirties who had come to Cheltenham sometime between 1901 and 1905 with her mother, to run the Food Reform Depot in Clarence Street.[3] They had previously run a restaurant in Limehouse, London, which continued to be run by her sister Charlotte after they left. Food Reform was effectively what we could call vegetarianism: it held that meat was responsible for many illnesses which could be helped or cured by switching to a vegetarian diet. This was a cause with which many suffragettes, particularly in Cheltenham, identified. It could, of course, be linked to the national concern about the health of the nation which was high on the Liberal government's agenda, as we saw in Chapter 2.

In 1906, the Food and Health Reform Society was formed in Cheltenham and Miss Eamonson became its honorary secretary. It appears that there may have been a pre-existing Vegetarian Society founded by Dr and Mrs Edward Wilkins.[4] He was a stockbroker and they lived on Queen's Road before moving to Sydenham Grove. Both were keen WFL supporters and she represented the WFL on deputations. It was among members of the WFL that the belief was particularly strong. We have already seen that Mrs Despard became a convert to vegetarianism and a small knot of Cheltenham women (and men) were similarly passionate. In late 1908 what claimed to be the first vegetarian hotel in England was opened in Winchcomb Street by Mrs Lisa Gard, a member of the WFL. Mrs Gard was a dressmaker according to the 1901 census, living with her husband John, an insurance agent who was nearly twice her age. However, in December 1908, she opened a small hotel 'with (its) light, airy and cheerful rooms, excellent sanitation and general convenience' and invited a number of people to celebrate with a luncheon of soups, savouries, sweets and cheese (*Looker-On* 12/12/08). The guest list demonstrates the close ties with the women's suffrage movement: it included Miss Bardsley (WFL who ran a Food Reform guest house later), Mme Borowikowski (sic), Dr and Mrs Earengey, Mrs and Miss Mills, Mrs Prust-Teague (Mme Borovikovsky's mother, also a supporter), Mrs Swiney and Dr and Mrs Wilkins (see above). During 1909, WFL meetings were held at the hotel but at some stage Mrs Gard left for London, where she appeared to have defected to a career in astrology in Bayswater!

---

3   Ruth Eamonson was to maintain her Food Reform stance – in 1939, she was still registered as a Food Reform shopkeeper and seemed to own a health food store in Oxford High Street while living in New Barn Lane, Prestbury.

4   This is evidenced in a 1932 *Cheltenham Chronicle* article which says that the society had been in existence for about forty years. Another report suggests that they both helped to found the town's Anti-Vivisection Society.

FOOD REFORM GUEST HOUSE,
SNOWDON,
LONDON ROAD, CHELTENHAM.

Five minutes from Town or Beautiful Country

SPECIALITY IN CONSERVATIVE COOKING.

Diets provided under doctors' orders.

MISS BARDSLEY.

Advertisement for the Food Reform establishment run by Miss Bardsley of the WFL. Vegetarianism was closely associated with the women's suffrage movement in some areas, Cheltenham being one of those. (*Cheltenham Chronicle* and others, regularly advertised over the last few years before 1914)

The link of vegetarianism to concern for overall health is also seen in Miss Eamonson and Miss Boult's classes for Swedish Gymnastics. From her house in College Road, Miss Boult ran remedial/gymnastic classes of various kinds and initially she was helped by Miss Eamonson. They both appear in the 1914 Report of the Gymnastic Teacher Suffrage Association, Miss Boult as having qualified at Anstey College and Miss Eamonson at Chelsea Polytechnic. Miss Winifred Boult was also a pupil at North London Collegiate School and would just have overlapped Florence How's (Earengey) time there, so there is much interweaving of individuals and interests which all came together in the Cheltenham WFL.

However, it can be seen that Miss and Mrs Mills and Mrs Swiney of the WSS were supportive of Food Reform too. It is generally thought that there was less 'New Age' fervour among the suffragists than among their more militant fellows. But vegetarianism was of interest to some, as was Theosophy which Mrs Swiney

---

5   Also Agnes Bales – see second Cheltenham prisoner section below – and Misses Boult and Eamonson.

LING'S SWEDISH GYMNASTICS.

THE MISSES BOULT and EAMONSON hold C.asses for Ladies and Children.

REMEDIAL EXERCISES given privately for cases of Flat Chest, Spinal Curvature, Flat Feet, Anæmia, Imperfect Breathing, &c.

For terms apply FINTRAY, College Road

Advertisement for the gymnastic classes run by Miss Eamonson and Miss Boult of the WFL. Gymnastics classes of this kind were linked to the campaign for 'health reform'. (*Cheltenham Chronicle* and others, regularly advertised over the last few years before 1914)

espoused.[5] With its basis in the spirituality of Hinduism, it naturally encouraged vegetarianism. Moreover, it encouraged equality of self-expression and leadership, so providing the links between philosophy, ethics and political action.

There was a strong connection to the Ethical Society of which Dr Callaway (WSS) and Dr Earengey were both leading lights and Miss Eamonson was on the committee. Lectures on Food Reform and ethics were often on the society's programme and the cruelties of killing animals (and indeed of vivisection) were emphasised. This could be seen as a feminist attack on a 'macho' culture of killing animals. The memorial service which the Cheltenham branch of the Ethical Society held for Mrs McIlquham is fascinating in the way in which a number of ideas of female equality, ethical considerations and a 'pure' lifestyle come together.

The address was by Dr Callaway, although read by Dr Earengey because he had a severe cold and could not attend. The service has a quasi-religious tone, with appropriate hymns being sung and readings from Job, St Matthew and the Persian Scriptures. The address paid tribute to the part Mrs McIlquham played in setting up the society, her generosity to its funds and her hard work and encouragement. And then the key part: 'Her religion was to follow truth and do good. For the old idea of the service of God she substituted the service of man. Our friend believed that true service to humanity paid no regard to sex distinctions. She was a strong opponent of the ancient theological dogma of the inferiority of woman.' He was at

81

pains to refute the need for a woman like Mrs McIlquham to pay heed to orthodox religious creeds – 'such a life as hers is another refutation of the delusion that belief in orthodox creeds is necessary for the good life.' Dr Earengey also referred to the 'natural sympathy between the ethical movement and that for the equality of the sexes'. The fact that Mrs McIlquham had an orthodox Church of England funeral service and burial adds to the rather curiously mixed tone of the Ethical Society's own memorial service.

The women's suffrage – vegetarianism battle in Cheltenham, Dr Burn v. Dr Garrett

As we have seen, women's suffrage supporters from across the spectrum supported Food Reform or vegetarianism. They were given a 'cause celebre' in 1913 when Dr Alice Burn, a member of the WSPU, got into dispute with Dr Garrett, the Chief Medical Officer for the town. This was ostensibly about her attitude to vegetarianism.

Dr Burn was a New Zealander who had qualified as a doctor in 1907 at Edinburgh and Glasgow. She had been one of the first six school medical inspectors in Co. Durham, employed to check the health of the future generation under the Liberal government's Act of 1907. While there, she had been actively involved in the WSPU, speaking frequently at meetings in Durham and Newcastle-upon-Tyne. At some stage, she was also resident school medical officer at Wycombe Abbey Girls' School. In 1912, she moved to Cheltenham, partly because she saw it as a place to educate her daughter who had previously had to be sent to a boarding school. She was described by the *Examiner* (03/12/12) as 'the wife of a professional man in New Zealand, incapacitated for remuneration' but at no time is there any further mention of her husband so we do not know whether he was in England. Although she was the sole bread-winner, she was prepared for the sake of 'more agreeable conditions' for a parent and child, to take a cut of £50 in salary to take up the post of Cheltenham's Assistant Schools Medical Officer and Assistant Medical Officer of Health at the rate of £250 p.a.

As a New Zealander, she had witnessed women being given the vote in 1893 after a petitioning campaign inspired by those in Britain and elsewhere. She therefore found it strange that the 'colonial master' was so reluctant to do the same. And she was said to have found English social problems which she encountered difficult to understand. So this was a woman whose women's suffrage beliefs were combined with a wider sense of social justice, garnered partly from her experience as a medical inspector in deprived areas of the North East.

The dispute in the town which led to Dr Burn losing her job centred on whether her advocacy of vegetarianism outside working hours needed permission from Dr Garrett, the Chief Medical Officer. This then led to disputes about the nature of free speech but it was complicated by local political concerns, such as whether the town would lose its grant from the Board of Education to help with its medical work. But there were underlying issues: in one of his letters which he made public, Dr Garrett referred to Dr Burn as a suffragette. This suggests antagonism between them on more than one count.

The trouble had surfaced in April 1913 when Dr Garrett complained about Dr Burn's active work in connection with vegetarianism. She objected strongly and told the Medical Sub-Committee that she refused his right to dictate to her on a matter outside her official duties. Not a lady to be trifled with, her staunch defence of her position was not something which the somewhat unpredictable and bristly Dr Garrett expected. Exchanges of letters and accusations continued through the summer when the sub-committee decided to take the matter to the Chief Medical

Dr Alice Burn of Cheltenham WSPU, Assistant Schools Medical Officer, who lost her job as a result of her vegetarian and other radical views. (The *Cheltenham Looker-On*, 10 January 1914)

Officer of the Board of Education, Sir George Newman, for advice. He advised that an assistant officer could not be allowed to express her views on matters such as Food Reform without the consent of the chief officer. She should apologise to Dr Garrett and give assurance that she would work loyally for him in the future. This she was not prepared to do, because she felt that her actual duties were not affected by what she did in her own time.

Dr Garrett's response was to urge Dr Burn's removal from her post and he had stated that he would resign if this did not happen. His bluff was called and his resignation had been accepted, to end his work on 24 December. However, the matter was referred to the Education Committee whose lengthy deliberations and acrimonious debate are well-recorded in the local press. In the account of the meeting of early December, the debate was attended by 'about 85 of the general public, most of them being ladies' including Dr Burn, and by Rev. J.H. Smith, the Unitarian minister and strong supporter of women's suffrage. He had addressed an ILP meeting the previous evening and had asked for support for Dr Burn. Some listeners were undoubtedly from the women's suffrage movement and there were frequent interruptions from the public section, causing the chairman to demand that this stop.

It is clear that there was no question of the excellent work being done by Dr Burn among the poorer schoolchildren of the town – this was not disputed. The characters of both her and Dr Garrett were put under some scrutiny and even a supporter of Dr Burn, Councillor Mann, said that 'the letters of Dr Garrett and Dr Burn were no credit to educated people' (*Chronicle* 06/12/13). It is implied that she was a lady who was not prepared to be conciliatory but Dr Garrett appeared to have been difficult to work with, was full of his own importance and had tendered his resignation at least once before![6]

When a second full meeting of the Education Committee was held, Dr Burn and 'a group of suffragette and vegetarian ladies and gentlemen' were present in the public area and a petition was read from about 300 local people asking for the retention of both Dr Garrett and Dr Burn by separating the two posts so that there was no question of Dr Burn having to be subservient to Dr Garrett. Although

---

6   Indeed, in the previous year, Dr Garrett had caused much debate and his temporary resignation by insisting on certain terms for the appointment of the first full-time Assistant Schools Medical Officer. Many of the councillors on the Education Committee felt that he was difficult to work with. Dr Earengey was a councillor on the Education Committee at this point and he defended Dr Garrett's position as logical and sensible – his clear and fair legalistic mind, as recalled above by his grandson, gave support to a man whom he was later to attack when he felt Dr Burn was being unfairly treated.

Dr Burn was present, her letter to the committee was read out after a resolution was put that she be dismissed from her post. She catalogued Dr Garrett's charges against her, which seem to have altered over the course of the dispute, and challenged his views and the way she had been denied information and a hearing. She also put the very fundamental point: 'Dr Garrett holds certain views with regard to food values; I hold others. Dr Garrett claims that his are the "accepted and usual views"; I claim that mine are sane and scientific and backed by weighty modern medical testimony.' But she referred to 'extraneous issues' now being dragged into the dispute which may well have referred to her WSPU activities.

Again, loud applause from Dr Burn's supporters caused the chairman to intervene and the reporter to note that Inspector Corbett and 'two of the most stalwart constables in the local force' were ready in the corridor for any disturbances! The reputation of WFL members for attracting disturbance had gone before them. The debate was just as bitter as the previous one, with a very clear division of opinion among the committee members. For example, one member thought Dr Burn would never submit herself to any living creature, and another that she had done 'injudicious things … and made them the laughing stock of everybody', whereas others emphasised the high regard she was held in by teachers and mothers. Again, it was said that Dr Garrett had been troublesome ever since he was appointed and that they 'had almost lost count of his many resignations'. Nevertheless, by a narrow majority, it was decided to dismiss her, not him (*Chronicle* 20/12/13).

The dismissal caused outrage, particularly among the women's suffrage supporters. For example, Miss Andrews, who was then secretary of the local WSPU and recently retired from her post at Cheltenham Ladies' College, wrote to the *Chronicle* deploring the defeat of the principle of freedom of speech. It is evident that she had been one of those at the crucial meeting. She suggested that, in the voting, all the women on the committee had voted to retain Dr Burn (but there were only two of them!) and she makes it very much a feminist issue. 'All men are agreed that the education of the child is specially woman's sphere,' an argument that had led to many insisting that schools medical officers were women (*Chronicle* 03/01/14).

Even more outrage was expressed in a protest meeting held at Montpellier Baths, chaired by Dr Earengey. Dr Burn was there to put her case and, ever the lawyer, Dr Earengey stated that she had been denied the right of defence. She implied that even the first few months under Dr Garrett had been difficult, with him giving her no assistance in her new role. He had never visited a school with her. She denied that she was autocratic or a difficult person to work with, and she cleverly challenged his opposition to her vegetarian views, demonstrating that his opposition to her was on other grounds too:

Till she came to Cheltenham she was never associated in any way with vegetarianism as such. When he accused her of having heretical opinions, she had always replied that he must blame her mother, who had brought her up in a certain manner. She knew the value of foods from an economic aspect, but until Dr Garrett wrote to the Press what she felt to be a very unfair and discourteous letter describing her as a vegetarian and militant suffragette and various other things, so far as she knew not ten people in the town were aware that she was a non-flesh eater.

(*Chronicle* 10/01/14)

The statement by Dr Burn suggests that she had not been attracted to Cheltenham because of its strong women's suffrage–vegetarianism link. She also stated that she had never taught vegetarianism in school and that not one mother or teacher would have known her views. Therefore, she had in no way made her views public within the context of her job.

The reference in Dr Garrett's letter to her being a 'militant suffragette' is significant. He had been angered in 1911 by the census protest organised by the militant groups, as he felt that the town would not get its borough status as a result and that this would damage the medical provision that could be given. In his 1912 annual report he reiterated this accusation, so he had obviously retained an anti-suffrage position. In his book of 1919, *From a Cotswold Height*, a book about walks in the area, one would have thought it impossible to air his prejudices. However, in a description of Cheltenham and its entertainments, he described the many halls and rooms available for meetings: 'for the constant effort and enterprise on the part of the populace, particularly of the feminine half, to find something creditable to do, whether on behalf of charity or instruction, or in advocacy of some special policy, cult or craze …' He doubtless included vegetarianism and women's suffrage within the 'cult or craze' categories!

Three councillors who were on the Education Committee gave speeches in her support and of a resolution condemning the Education Committee and Town Council for their denial of free speech to an employee. Sympathy for Dr Burn was also expressed by the *Looker-On* (10/01/14): the paper felt that she had not been allowed to express her opinion and so she was offered an interview. She put her views on the right not to be 'gagged' in her private time, but like Miss Andrews in her letter, she also emphasised that the work should be done by a woman – not only medically trained but also with a 'trained mother instinct which opens the door to much of the best knowledge'. The paper, which targeted the 'respectable' classes in Cheltenham, was courageous in its support for her.

Ironically, in a postscript to this lengthy episode of vitriolic exchanges, there was difficulty in appointing Alice Burn's successor. It was decided to give the post to Dr Janette Hill, but she declined the post when she found out about the conflict with Dr Garrett – apparently she had been 'informed' by someone who had sent her a newspaper report of one of the meetings! The post had to be given to a man but reservations were expressed by some on the committee about the desirability of a man examining young children, and whether mothers would have confidence in him – it was seen as a woman's job! The ensuing debate raked up many of the issues from the Burn-Garrett conflict – it would take time for wounds to heal.

The link between vegetarianism and women's suffrage had become a controversial one in the town, but that did not diminish the strength of either belief.

Another cause to fight – the Daisy Turner case

Again it was primarily, but not exclusively, the members of the WFL, with the support of Mrs Despard as its national figurehead, who tried to get public support behind a young Cheltenham girl, Daisy Turner. She was charged with murdering her newborn baby boy. This became a case about the moral responsibility of men and how far the law treated men differently from women, and it was therefore part of the wider fight for women's rights.

In June 1911, it was reported that a 19-year-old resident housemaid at St Mary's Hall Church of England Training College had given birth to a baby whose body was found in a drawer in her room. When she was observed by the lady superintendent to be 'unwell', she was sent home to be with her mother on Francis Street, Bath Road. The inquest returned the verdict of 'wilful murder' and suggested that Daisy had killed the baby with the heel of her shoe. It is significant that she was represented by Dr Earengey. When she appeared before the police court, Dr Earengey pressed unsuccessfully for the explanation that the baby had accidentally fallen.

The champions of women's rights now came to the fore in a campaign and letters to the press. Flora Kelley, the CUWFA secretary, set up a fund to support her while she was in prison awaiting trial. Ruth Eamonson of the WFL wrote that 'moral responsibility' should be shared – that there was some Cheltenham man who was guilty of making her a victim of his lust (*Echo* 14/07/11). In another letter, she must have named the man responsible because the paper put a row of dots and refused to be subject to a libel case (18/07/11). Apparently, Daisy Turner had told her aunt who the man responsible was – as she had left her post in service with Colonel Muir in The Park in March, one can speculate that the father of the baby might have been one of the household. Both Winifred Boult (WFL) and Miss Theodora Mills (WSS) these three women wrote letters of support to the papers, as did Mrs Kate McMurdo of the WSPU – all had also just evaded the census so were in militant mood.

In a show of unity, a letter to the *Looker-On* (15/07/11) was signed by the Rector of Cheltenham, Francis L'Estrange-Fawcett, and his wife, Major-General and Mrs Swiney of the WSS, Miss E.L. Andrews, the local WSPU secretary, Flora Kelley, the honorary secretary of the CUWFA, Florence Earengey, secretary of the WFL, together with three lady doctors, Dr Billings, Dr Cargill and Dr Harrison, all women's suffrage supporters, and Constance Ferguson who was WSPU secretary for a while. Also listed were the wife of a surgeon, Laura McCraith-Blakeney (WSS) and the young wife of Rev. Noott of Berkeley Street. The letter pointed out that Daisy Turner had been incarcerated when she was still very unwell after the birth and was thus mentally and physically unfit to give evidence, that she was imprisoned in harsh conditions and that nobody represented her at the autopsy. The emphasis was on the need for changes in the administration of the law and on the need to give expression to 'the woman's point of view'.

The anti-suffragists, however, also made it clear that the women were not using 'common sense'. Mrs Colquhoun at a public meeting of the National League for Opposing Women's Suffrage in July (*Looker-On*, 22 July 1911) dealt with the case at length and suggested that the letters to the press had ignored the facts about prison regulations. She implied was that Daisy Turner was not badly treated. She also rebutted the arguments that the man should be charged too, as it was not a crime to have a child but it was a crime to murder it. She was here evading the question of whether Daisy Turner's baby had been born as the result of rape, which was implied by some of the letters.

The WFL held another meeting in the Town Hall just before the trial began. An appeal had been made to Mrs Despard for support. The subject of the meeting, 'The Unmarried Mother', was a clear message of what was uppermost in the organisers' minds and Mrs Despard gave a passionate address on how the unmarried mother was in law solely responsible for her child, while a married woman was not. Miss Mills asked a question about the Daisy Turner case, but Mrs Despard said that it was 'sub judice' so she could not discuss it. However, she did say what noble work Dr Earengey was doing in her defence!

The trial was attended by women's suffrage supporters including Mrs Despard. Dr Earengey had instructed one of the best barristers in the district to defend Daisy and he did well in convincing the jury that no one could prove that the baby was alive when it was born, so it could not be a case of murder. Daisy was found guilty of concealment of a birth but, as she had already been in prison for four months, she was given a notional one day's imprisonment but immediately discharged. Again, the wider concerns of the women's movement had been expressed through practical action by Cheltenham followers.

6

MILITANCY AND THE CENSUS BOYCOTT

The WFL ploughs a separate furrow

While the campaign for Daisy Turner gained broad support from women's suffrage supporters, during this period the local WFL had decided to sever its ties with the WSS and establish its distinct identity. It was reported at the end of 1910 that Mrs How Earengey and nine others had now decided to work only for the WFL and the symbol of this is a picture of Mrs Earengey, her sister Miss Bardsley and Miss Boult with the WFL banner campaigning in the December 1910 general election. There is no indication of why the break was decided: nothing had happened nationally to precipitate it but there may have been some local disagreement. Or Mrs Earengey might have decided that the WFL was in danger of losing its identity?

Cheltenham WFL leaders campaigning for the December 1910 election: (left to right) Mrs Florence Earengey, Miss Bardsley and Miss Boult. (*Cheltenham Chronicle and Gloucestershire Graphic*, 10 December 1910)

WOMEN'S FREEDOM LEAGUE SALE OF WORK, TOWN HALL, CHELTENHAM, NOVEMBER 29, 1910.

Miss Bales, Miss Eamonson, Miss Boult (treasurer), Miss Bardsley, Miss Howe, Mrs. Earengey (hon. secretary), Miss Earengey, The Mayoress (Mrs. Margrett), Mrs. Gard (Kyrea the Palmist), Mrs. Nicholls, Miss Margaret Sidley (London).

Cheltenham WFL Sale of Work, the key figures in the branch pose with the mayoress, who was sympathetic to the women's movement. (*Cheltenham Chronicle and Gloucestershire Graphic*, 3 December 1910)

This stand did not in practice mean an end to all co-operation, as seen in the last chapter. Also, Dr Earengey remained a WSS supporter and actually chaired the meeting when his wife's departure was announced!

During 1910–11, the WFL continued to hold At Homes with subjects such as 'The Military Training of Women', a remarkably prescient topic. However, one wonders how far membership was affected by the decision to demand allegiance to the WFL alone. A picture of WFL members at their Sale of Work (CCGG 03/12/10) shows those women already mentioned as key figures above, apart from Miss Agnes Bales who was to make her name in 1913 and Mrs Evelyn Heller Nicholls of Glencairn Park Road, whose husband was a music teacher at Dean Close School. With no membership lists to consult, one has to go on press reports and the signatures in the 1912 book (see final chapter) which suggests a tightly-knit core of perhaps only sixteen women. If this is so, it makes their achievements all the more remarkable. The reputation of Mrs How Earengey, and of her husband, gave the group prominent status within the town and her insistence that the WFL should be heard is seen in her frequent letters to the press.

However, when the WFL women decided to separate themselves, they were the only militant group in Cheltenham as the previous attempt to establish the WSPU had failed. This was to change in early 1911, with the arrival of a full-time salaried WSPU organiser to galvanise the town into action. So when the WFL launched their campaign to persuade women to boycott the census of 1911, they assumed they would be at the forefront of local organisation. The census campaign provides an insight into the strength of militancy in the town and the relationship between the WSPU and the WFL.

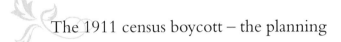

The 1911 census boycott – the planning

During 1910, a conciliation bill (produced by a cross-party committee), which would have given about one million women the vote, was progressing slowly through Parliament and there were doubts about Asquith's intentions. These doubts proved to be justified when, in the late summer, he announced that he would not give the bill any more parliamentary time. Women's anger was fuelled by this and

A cartoon attacking Prime Minister Asquith's shelving of the Conciliation Bill, a measure which would have given about one million women the vote. (*Punch*, 20 July 1910)

it built upon pre-existing secret WFL discussions about the government's census plans. It was known that more personal details would be required than in previous censuses, although the exact nature of these was not known when the WFL began to consider a boycott. Mrs Despard was increasingly taken with Gandhi's philosophy of passive resistance to unjust laws and the census boycott fell within this definition.

Edith How Martyn, by now the Head of the WFL Political and Militant Department, was at the centre of the planning for the boycott. She approached the other women's suffrage groups for support and asked them to send delegates to a secret conference. The request had a mixed response but, in the meantime, she had consulted her brother-in-law, Dr Earengey, on the legality of such a response to the census bill. Cheltenham therefore had a major role in the planning of the nationwide campaign.

The resistance policy was not publicly announced until after the King's Speech in February 1911: it had been agreed that, if the speech made no mention of a measure to enfranchise women, the plans would be put into action. Already WFL delegates (including representation from Cheltenham but no names are known) had come to London aware of what was being mooted. The WFL was further inflamed by revelations of the census questions about length of marriage, number of children alive and dead, and women's occupations. They argued that these questions could be used by the government to make assumptions about infant mortality and so limit women's labour in the lower classes. Many felt that the questions were an insensitive intrusion into women's lives.

Edith How Martyn thundered in the pages of *The Vote* (11/02/11) that:

It is clearly evident that Suffragists (sic) must change their grievance from an inconvenience to a menace. Any government which refuses to recognise women must be met by women's refusal to recognize the Government …

Is it to be expected that we shall without protest or hindrance fill in Census papers and thus assist and make easy the task of governing women while denying them the elementary rights of citizenship?

The WSPU had initially hesitated about the idea of a boycott but now came out in full support and began to organise their own members. This coincided with the decision to send an organiser to Cheltenham to attempt to establish a branch. Miss Ada Flatman arrived in late January 1911.

In Cheltenham, there were now two forceful figures trying to organise a census boycott, Florence Earengey and Ada Flatman. Some friction emerged between them; letters to the *Examiner* in February and early March showed each was anxious to show that she was in charge of her own census campaign. There seems to have been no attempt to co-ordinate their efforts. In fact, in the *Echo* letters page (28/03/11), Mrs Earengey objected to the suggestion that the WSPU was breaking new ground in the town:

> Anyone who knows Cheltenham must be aware of the fact that long before the arrival of WSPU upon the scene of action, the inhabitants of this town had had opportunities of enlightenment on the question of 'Votes for Women', and these opportunities were not let slip, for cannot Cheltenham claim as peculiarly her own the magnificent pioneer work and influence of Mrs McIlquham and Mrs Swiney?

However, it seems to have been the WSPU who mounted the more high-profile campaign with a particularly noteworthy meeting on 28 March, just before the 2 April census day, when Mrs Pethick-Lawrence, the honorary treasurer of the

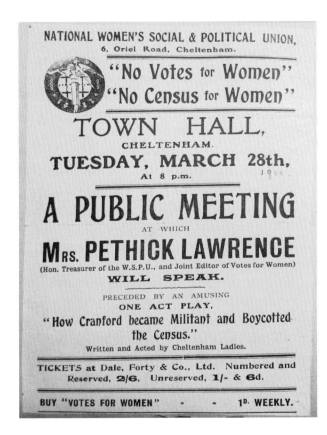

Poster advertising a WSPU meeting in Cheltenham which was being held primarily to gain support for boycotting the 1911 census. (Suffragette Fellowship Archive © Museum of London)

WSPU and joint editor (and source of finance!) of *Votes for Women*, the weekly paper of the union, addressed a meeting. Annie Kenney, the 'mill-girl' who was close to the Pankhursts and at this point was a paid organiser in Bristol, was also advertised. Sadly, press accounts of the meeting do not reveal who were the local women who wrote and performed the accompanying play, *How Cranford Became Militant and Boycotted the Census*.

Annie Kenney suggested in her address from the chair that the meeting was not only to press the government to grant time for a Women's Suffrage Bill, but to call attention to their proposed census boycott which had received virtually no publicity from the London press. This was a somewhat misleading claim, as there had been much bitter controversy in the national papers about the wisdom or otherwise of the boycott. It was reflected in the pages of the Cheltenham papers, so most would be aware of what was being planned. The WSS stalwart, Dr Charles Callaway, took to the letters pages to denounce the tactic, accusing its supporters of being unpatriotic. He echoed the prominent criticism of Professor Michael Sadler, a Liberal academic who advocated the use of well-researched data such as census data as the basis of social reform. *The Times* published Sadler's famous letter which argued that a boycott would be 'a crime against science' and, in a phrase calculated to enrage suffragists and suffragettes alike, 'a nursery fit of bad temper' (14/02/11). Just as Edith How Martyn, as a fellow scientist, rebutted his criticism with the suggestion that politicians juggled with statistics to suit their own theories, so her sister Florence Earengey rebutted Dr Callaway's attack (*Echo* 31/03/11):

> That this protest will invalidate the Census statistics is perfectly true, but the men and women who are making the protest consider that to give information upon which future legislation affecting women will be based is to be consenting parties to women's position of subjection under the present law.
>
> The hands of social reformers are weakened and will remain so as long as the community does not avail itself of every possible means of solving social problems, and this it cannot be said to do while it hampers half the community with artificial restrictions.

Dr Callaway, ever the gentleman and a former colleague of Mrs Earengey in the WSS, replied that he agreed with Mrs Earengey's principles and had usually refrained from criticising militant methods 'out of regard to the views of Mrs Earengey and other friends'. But he still felt that militant policy alienated many good friends to the cause and that refusing to comply with the census demands would inflict 'an injury upon the community at large'.

His reply was much more conciliatory than the letter of Ludwig Stern, a German gentleman living in Charlton Kings,[1] who contrasted the firm hand taken by the German authorities towards women's demands with what he saw happening in Britain. He accused Mrs Earengey of lacking 'local patriotism' and of 'pure and simple anarchy' (*Echo* 03/04/11). He was partly appalled by the failure of the appeal to the WFL and others by the mayor, Alderman Margrett, to call of their protest. The mayor wanted the census to show that Cheltenham had a population of over 50,000 so that it could be made a county borough. This he thought would enhance the financial status of the town and would therefore benefit all ratepayers. As Charles Margrett and his wife were sympathetic to women's suffrage, he probably expected co-operation.[2]

Interestingly, in light of his future opposition to Dr Burn of the WSPU (see last chapter), Dr Garrett, the Medical Officer of Health, also launched an attack on the protest. He likened the act of 'anarchy' with the blowing up of the Town Hall when full of people, including suffragists! In other words, they would be harming many people's interests as well as their own – but the comparison is somewhat immoderate (*Echo* 01/04/11). He also seemed to suggest that the WFL members were blindly following Mrs Despard and not exercising individual thought.

The debate in the local press certainly publicised the planned protest. The *Examiner* of 1 March published a letter from Ada Flatman, saying that there had been many offers of houses for the resisters to stay in and her address was given as 6 Oriel Road, so it was possible for anyone to see who to contact.

What happened on census night?

What happened on 2 April? It is clear that there were separate pockets of WFL and WSPU resisters with some houses being used as 'collecting points'. For the WFL, these were Miss Bardsley's Food Reform Guest House (Snowdon), and Miss

---

1   Living at Elm Villa, Charlton Kings (six rooms), he was a recently married 50-year-old teacher of languages, working from home, with his wife.

2   It should be noted that there was a possibility that the Original Company brewery workers and their families would also boycott the census, in order to ensure that the town was not given county borough status. This was because every licensed premises would face an increase in the cost of their licence if this were to occur. Subsequent press reports suggest that, according to the manager, some had left town in order not to be counted in Cheltenham.

Boult's house, Fintray, College Road. For the WSPU, they were Bedford Lodge, College Road, where Miss Flatman stayed, and next-door Lindley, the home of Mrs Angus. Thus there were at least three houses in College Road at the centre of the protest.

The account of census night by Miss Flatman in an interview with an *Echo* reporter is entertaining, while not revealing much real detail (03/04/11). Headed 'DETECTIVE'S ALL-NIGHT VIGIL. THEY FIDDLE WHILE HE FREEZES', the interview took place after she had returned to her own apartments, having remained absent until midday so that she could not be included on the census return:

> We have had rather an exciting time. Evidently they know that we are a dangerous people, for we were very closely watched.
>
> A good friend lent me her house in her absence for the weekend, asking no questions, and that made me pro.tem. the legal occupier.
>
> I and another friend sallied forth on Sunday evening to take up residence, and we were immediately shadowed by detectives, who sprang from some area steps where they had no doubt spent a very pleasant part of a wet Sunday watching for the ringleaders to show them the way to the Suffragist Mecca. This we did not in the least mind doing, knowing that the majority of our part were already awaiting our arrival.
>
> We parried the detectives some time, first walking in one direction and then in another, sometimes holding long conversations at street corners. At last I held them at bay while my friend disappeared down a side street. Then I hid myself behind a corner where a detective immediately passed by, thinking to follow me.
>
> I advanced and asked him why he was following me, and we had a little conversation. I told him I knew his reason was that he wanted to find out our destination which was very silly, but still he might do so. I afterwards went to my house, but lost sight of my shadower. We had delayed making for the house at once in order to let the rest of the party get there.
>
> At the house we had a blaze of light, for we did not want to hide the fact that we were there, and any officer passing would know that unusual things were taking place, as in many other houses in the neighbourhood (College-road).
>
> It was necessary, though, in some cases to keep the house in absolute darkness; and there were many hiding in houses which were never suspected. Thus the numbers will never be known.
>
> From this point of view it exceeded my expectation. We have not been in Cheltenham long, and the people have been aroused to the thing and have

responded very well indeed to our demands. I cannot tell you the exact numbers, or even give any idea of the number of houses put at our disposal, because that is part of our secret.

We were sitting up to the small hours of the morning, hoping of course that the poor detective whiled away his time listening to the violin solos and peals of laughter of the merry Suffragettes.

In the early hours of the morning, the Suffragettes tracked their tracker to a newspaper shop, where he bought literature to assist him in passing away the time. He was blue with the cold. Those of us who wanted to leave left quietly, while others remained in the house until mid-day.

The detective stayed watching till 10.30 a.m. I then left the house myself, and had a conversation with him, telling him how sorry I was that he had had such a long wait in the cold, and that if he remained all day and another night he would not be able to count. He replied that he did not want to count: but we wondered why he had been watching us all those hours.

I filled in the schedule for the house with the words 'As women do not count politically, I and the guests in my house refuse to be counted for the census,' and signed it with my own name.

If the Mayor and Town Council will get a pledge from the Prime Minister for full facilities for our Bill this session, we will willingly give the information which has been withheld, so that they may know the full population of Cheltenham for the purposes of making it a county borough.

The only other details to emerge from the night are in a rather tongue-in-cheek account in the *Chronicle* of 8 April where the sympathies of the writer are hard to discern. He speculated that these must have been 'exceedingly cosy affairs' with all the amenities of the fashionable 'at homes' with 'nice society, delectable catering, music, cards, even the companionship of cultured and sympathetic gentlemen'. One male head of a family had allegedly told the writer that he had a 'very nice time'. He also told the reporter that it was a very mild protest but 'quite a number of us felt very much regret at having to make this or any other protest'. The reporter understood that some household heads refused to co-operate while some merely entered the number of persons in the house. Again, these are not very insightful revelations but, in the absence of personal reminiscences, they are all we have.

Who took part in the protest?

By searching the census returns for known Cheltenham suffragist/suffragette names in 1911, and by using the 1901 census for cross-referencing (and reasonable deductions on occasions), it is possible to pinpoint who evaded the census or made some kind of defiant statement. It should be remembered that these women (and potentially their husbands) were defying the law and there was a fine of £5 or one month's imprisonment for the offence. In taking this action, women were risking the disapproval of 'polite' Cheltenham society and bringing disgrace on their families. In the end, the government was unwilling and unable to pursue the evaders but the women did not know this would be the outcome.

The first group of evaders below are important as the NUWSS had not given their support at national level.

WSS

Mrs Ruth Mills and Miss Theodora Mills (both of Lowmandale, Leckhampton Road) – do not appear in the census at all. I cannot find the schedule for their house so any servant(s) must have also been absent. However, I cannot find the house listed

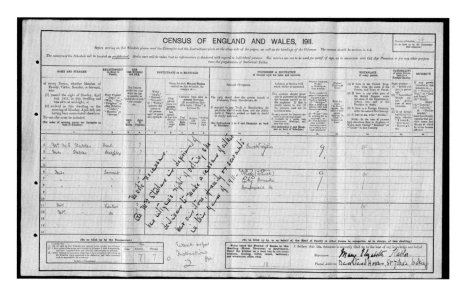

The 1911 census return for Mrs Mary Stables, a former Cheltenham resident and WSS member who had moved to Woking. Her protest reads: 'No Vote No Census. As Mrs. Stables if deprived of her citizen's right of voting, she declines to make a return of either her visitors, family or servants in the year of 1911.' (GBC-1911-RG14-03044-0153)

on the enumerator's summary lists either. This is odd – unless he was trying to avoid having to confess to a problem in obtaining information, but he could have recorded an empty house.

Mrs Rosa Frances Swiney (of Sandford Lawn, Bath Road) – does not appear on the census. Her husband provided the requisite information about the length of their marriage, number of children, etc.

Another possible evader is *Mrs Laura McCraith Blakeney.* She was a WSS supporter and in 1911 the house which she shared with her surgeon husband at 5 Crescent Terrace was occupied only by her 6-year-old son and three servants, one of whom was described as a children's nurse. They cannot be found elsewhere. The complete absence of either parent is perhaps unlikely.

Mrs Mary Stables – in Cheltenham until *c.*1910, she protested in Woking. She had lived at 2 College Lawn and had been an active member of the WSS between at least 1902 and 1909, including speaking at public meetings and garden parties. Before moving to Cheltenham, she had lived in the pleasant suburbs of Leeds with her husband, who was a tea dealer. Her two children lived with her in Cheltenham and her son Harold, a barrister, appeared on a Cheltenham WSS platform in 1912. Ties with the town had obviously been retained.

Hers is an example of where the woman refused to complete the form and wrote a protest across it, but the enumerator has managed to obtain some information, perhaps by intimidating one of the servants since their roles in the household are listed.

WFL

Miss C. Bardsley and one servant (Snowdon, Sydenham Villas), *Dr Edward Wilkins, Mrs Emmeline Wilkins.* Miss Bardsley and Dr and Mrs Wilkins plus one domestic servant are listed by the enumerator, who has not elicited any more details about age, occupation, place of birth, etc. Dr Wilkins is titled Mr Wilkins here. The signature does not seem to be Miss Bardsley's. Again, the enumerator was perhaps gaining his knowledge from local information about the Food Reform Guest House.

Mrs L. Borovikovski – cannot be found nor can her son Sergei, by then 7 years old.

Miss Agnes Bales (of 5 Blenheim Place, Bath Road) – she was not registered with her parents although we know she was still living there in 1913. Her father does declare that he has one living child.

Miss Winifred Boult and one servant, Miss Ruth Eamonson – at Fintray, College Road on that night. Again, filled in by the enumerator, the two women were named, perhaps using local knowledge but incorrectly putting Miss Boult as 'Mrs' and married.

The 1911 census return for the Earengey household, Ashley Rise, Battledown. The statement, probably written by the enumerator, reads: 'The other members of this household were away as a protest against women having no parliamentary vote.' (GBC-1911-RG14-15578-0161)

Miss Lilian How, sister of Florence Earengey. She was then living with her parents at Torrington, Western Road. She is not to be found anywhere.

Mrs Florence Earengey and her daughter Oenone aged 7, then living at Ashley Rise, Battledown. Presumably, Dr Earengey could not put his professional status at risk so he had filled in his own details, but it looks as though he (or she?) had erased the details of length of marriage, children, etc. The statement written across the page underneath his entry is not in his handwriting but reads: 'The other members of this household were away as a protest against women having no parliamentary vote.'[3]

Mrs Evelyn Heller Nicholls of 1 Glencairn Park Road. She was married to a Professor of Music at Dean Close School and had one daughter aged 4. She is

---

3   It is possible that there was usually a domestic servant too? The house did have eleven rooms, so it was a considerable size for a middle-class woman to manage, but that does not necessarily mean that any domestic help was resident and the Earengeys were, for the period, a little unusual in their principles.

completely omitted from the form and does not appear anywhere else, but her husband William had declared that they had been married for eight years.

WSPU

Mrs Elizabeth Angus and her four daughters and four servants of Lindley, College Road. Another of the forms filled in by the enumerator as Mrs Angus did not sign it. She is named and then the word 'Daughter' is listed four times, followed by 'Servant' three times and then 'Governess'. Written across the form in pencil is 'Suffragettes'. Mrs Angus had been at the forefront of WSS committees in the town and had been a contributor to WSPU national funds in 1911. She was very much part of the relief efforts during the war while being part of the social scene, chaperoning her daughters at society balls. Eventually, it was reports of the latter which gave me her daughters' names and which enabled me to trace her to being Elizabeth, the 44-year-old widow of James Angus who had been a very wealthy coalmaster. When living in Ochiltree, Ayrshire, in 1901, they had seven servants! Her daughter's wedding in Leckhampton in 1920 was a society event. Interestingly, she was born in New Zealand, another like Alice Burn who may have found it difficult to understand why the mother country was not giving women the vote.

The society wedding of Jean Angus, the daughter of Mrs Elizabeth Angus, who was a WSPU activist and census evader in Cheltenham. As a widow head of household, she withheld the names of her four daughters and four servants who lived with her at Lindley, College Road. (The *Cheltenham Looker-On*, 10 July 1920)

Miss Ada Flatman together with one servant, one male and one female child and nine other females staying at Bedford Lodge, College Road, as described above. This was all filled in by the enumerator with no signature. The house belonged to Mrs Constance Fergus(s)on who was the new local WSPU secretary, but was away from the town for the census. She was one of the signatories in a letter about the Daisy Turner case later in the year. What is *not* on the schedule is the statement Miss Flatman claimed to the *Echo* reporter to have made on it. Whether the enumerator substituted another form for the original one is doubtful but possible. It is possible that Miss Flatman was making an exaggerated statement.

Mrs Amy Creese of Atherstone Lawn, Portland Street, had perhaps discussed with her husband Alfred, a fancy draper, how to handle the issue. The line of the form on which her name should have appeared has 'wife away' crossed out. She was definitely a WSPU supporter as she contributed to their funds that year.

Mr Alfred Dubbin and Mrs Olive Dubbin of 6 Bath Road, Paragon Parade, a few doors away from the Swineys, no record of any schedule. Alfred was a builder. She contributed to WSPU funds that year.

Mrs Catherine McMurdo of 2 Clarence Square. She contributed to WSPU funds that year and supported the Daisy Turner appeal. She was listed by her husband, George, a retired civil servant with the Irish Lighthouse Department, as Catherine, Wife, aged 52, but then the line is crossed out, by whom it is impossible to say! George was himself involved in causes such as anti-vivisection, so he may well have been sympathetic.

Mrs Mary Jane Margrett, her daughter Mrs Gladys Henegan and two female servants of Priory Lodge, High Street. Again, the form was filled in by the enumerator with the bare details and no signature. This was the Mrs H.G. Margrett who donated 2s 6d to WSPU funds later in the month. She was the widow of Henry George, an accountant/farmer, a councillor and brother of Mayor Charles Margrett, who had begged the women not to put in jeopardy Cheltenham's chance of being designated a county borough (see above). She had lived in the same eight-roomed house since sometime in the 1890s. Her daughter is also listed as a widow but, in fact, her husband Patrick Henegan (no occupation) was registered a few doors away in Priory Place with his mother, sister and a servant. One assumes Gladys was a sympathiser too and that is why she was with her mother rather than her husband.

Miss Gladys Daubeny/Mrs Gladys Mellersh became the new honorary secretary of the WSPU in 1912 and had given a generous donation the previous year. In a big society wedding in June 1911 she married William Lock Mellersh, a local solicitor, and they set up home at Bergholt, Painswick Road. Both she and her husband maintained their support for the movement. However, on census night, neither she

The wedding of Miss Gladys Daubeny and Mr William Mellersh. She evaded the census and, after her marriage, became secretary of Cheltenham WSPU. (The *Cheltenham Looker-On*, 17 June 1911)

nor her mother (or her sister) appear to be listed anywhere and, perhaps significantly, Gladys's father, Hugh, a retired Royal Navy gentleman, put no details of length of marriage or number of children on the schedule for Haddo, Pittville, which suggests some kind of agreement that this information should not be divulged.

Mrs Frances Stirling and Miss Elvira Stirling of 30 Clarence Square decided to give the required details but made it clear what their position was. Mrs Stirling wrote 'This Form is filled in through the magnanimity of a Suffragette. Hoping that a more generous and just Legislation for Women will soon be forthcoming from those in Power in Great Britain.' She describes herself as of Private Means, WSPU Suffragette, under the Occupation column and her daughter Elvira, aged 24, is described as Women's Suffrage WSPU worker. She is described in *Votes for Women* (14/04/11) as having 'dressed' the committee room window, for the by-election presumably at their High Street headquarters.[4]

---

4   Mrs Stirling's husband was a military gentleman and, as the children were all born in Canada, one can assume that this is where he met his Canadian wife.

The 1911 census return for the Stirling household (WSPU) in Cheltenham showing their census protest. (GBC-1911-RG14-15545-0325)

CUWFA

Mrs Alice Gardiner was married to Charles Irving Gardiner, who later showed his support for the cause through the CUWFA. He was a schoolmaster and in the schedule for 6 Paragon Parade he describes himself as married, but there is no reference to her or to the length of marriage, one of the required bits of information. He married Alice Ann Pearce in 1904, when she was a teacher of banjo, mandolin, guitar and balalaika at the Ladies' College – a lady of some talents!

Mrs Emily Gurney showed her support for women's suffrage the next year by signing the book of thanks to MP Agg-Gardner. In the schedule, her husband, Walter, a solicitor, included details of two children, a visitor and three servants living at 12 Wellington Square, but there are no details given of the length of marriage, etc. She does not appear anywhere else.

Mrs Beatrice Household was another person who signed the 1912 book of thanks to Agg-Gardner under the CUWFA heading. She was married to Horace, Secretary for Education to Gloucestershire County Council, and they were living at the twelve-roomed Park Lawn. Like the above men, he had filled in the form for himself, his young son and three servants, but the details of his marriage were crossed out quite forcefully, so denying the enumerator the finer details he required.

In each of the three last cases, the husband seems to have colluded in both the 'disappearance' of his wife and in refusing to give required information. In the other cases, we are sometimes alerted to evasion by the enumerator's attempts to give some information.[5] Those cases where a statement has been written on the form are particularly illuminating of the strength of feeling. Cheltenham women, and men, had certainly made a contribution to the campaign that had been initially headed by the ex-Cheltenham woman, the WFL's Edith How Martyn.

---

5   In contrast to some other areas where there were evasions or protests, I can find no comments by a frustrated enumerator on the summary sheets.

The WFL continues its fight – a second Cheltenham prisoner

After the census effort, the local WFL continued both its own meetings and some joint public meetings. Although Edith How Martyn had left the organisation in 1912 after falling out with Mrs Despard, her sister Mrs Earengey remained in the WFL and in 1912 was made local president. Miss Eamonson became secretary and Mme Borovikovsky honorary secretary – the impression of a small tightly-knit group is again reinforced. Meetings were held in Miss Bardsley's Food Reform Guest House and Mrs Despard returned to talk. Lilla How and Miss Boult represented the branch at an International Suffrage Fair in London. The branch joined with the WSS and CUWFA in a meeting to hear Sir John Cockburn, the ex-Premier of South Australia, and Mrs Philip Snowden, a Labour supporter, who urged the meeting to forget party politics for the sake of women's suffrage. More controversially, the two societies joined together for a meeting on 'The White Slave Traffic' (prostitution), a topic much discussed by women's groups at the time.

It was the WFL which hosted the visit to the town in May 1913 by the illustrator, poet and writer, Laurence Housman, whose brother was the more famous poet, A.E. Housman. Laurence and his sister Clemence were great supporters of the women's suffrage movement and he helped form the Men's League for Women's Suffrage in 1907. He claimed that his social conscience had been awakened by Mrs Pankhurst but, like others, he had become frustrated by her inability to consider another point of view, in particular her and Christabel's unwillingness to allow men to have any meaningful role in the campaign. More militant tactics such as arson worried him and so he became more aligned with the WFL. In his speech at the Town Hall he, perhaps inadvisedly, suggested that there were always some women whose temperament would not allow them to protest constitutionally when they had been enraged by injustice. Militancy was part of human nature! This was not an argument calculated to win support and it allowed Dr Blakeney, a surgeon, to propose a vote of thanks but to state that he thought that militancy was misguided. However, this was according to the *Chronicle*: the more sympathetic *Looker-On* emphasised the part of his speech which decried the way in which women had been subjected to 'bestial' treatment by the police and prison authorities.

But it was another court case which gave the WFL more publicity. On the night of 2 February 1913, three women from the WFL were arrested for placarding pillar boxes, although the WFL Annual Report says that five members were involved in the attempts! The three who were caught were familiar names – Miss Winifred Boult, Miss Ruth Eamonson and Miss Agnes Bales. PC Aston had seen Miss Boult

Laurence Housman, writer and journalist, who spoke in Cheltenham, wrote a women's suffrage play, *Alice in Ganderland*. It satirised the attitude of 'mad' politicians who resisted the idea of votes for women. (Author's collection, composition © Paul Jones)

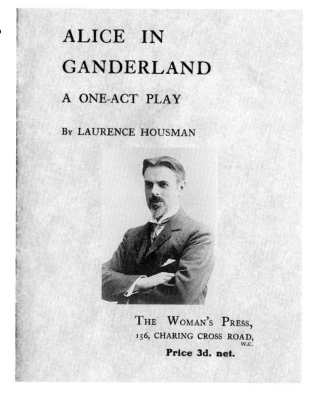

ALICE IN GANDERLAND

A ONE-ACT PLAY

By LAURENCE HOUSMAN

THE WOMAN'S PRESS,
156, CHARING CROSS ROAD, W.C.

Price 3d. net.

and Miss Bales in Sandford Road and discovered that a placard was fixed to the electric light standard, while in College Road he found one on a pillar box. He then saw them in Imperial Square in the act of fixing one to a pillar box. One of the defendants was carrying a Dorothy bag with ten more gummed placards and a sponge and water. The placards read:

> Dare to be free! Whereas the Prime Minister has egregiously failed to secure the fulfilment of his pledge to the Suffragists, they require nothing short of a Government measure for the enfranchisement of women. Failing such a measure, they intend to defy the Government and invite the people to rally to their support.
>
> (*Examiner* 06/03/13)

Hardly an inflammatory message as the prosecution maintained, nor a very punchy one! However, they were prosecuted under a section of the Post Office Act which was to prevent the slits of pillar boxes being obstructed. The fact that on 1 February

107

The postbox in College Road, Cheltenham, which was 'placarded' by WFL women in February 1913. Misses Boult and Bales were charged with an offence under the Post Office Act. (© Paul Jones)

the *Chronicle* declared, with little evidence, that adhesive gum had been poured into at least one pillar box in the town by the actions of 'suffragists' had probably put the police on alert. It was reported alongside accounts of suffragette use of fire and acid in Liverpool and Birmingham, so the reporter was accusing Cheltenham activists by association.[6]

When Agnes Bales and Winifred Boult appeared in court, Agnes Bales pointed out that their act was different from that of the 'very militant' section of the suffragettes who were engaged in the firing of pillar boxes – that was destruction of property, public and private. But they pleaded guilty. Each was fined 10s or their goods would be distrained to that value if they refused to pay. Fourteen days' imprisonment was the alternative. Both said they had no goods to be distrained and they refused to pay. Agnes Bales declared that she lived with her parents so that she had 'no special property', i.e. nothing of her own. She was employed as clerk to a fine art publisher and was in her mid-thirties by then, but her father was a domestic gardener and she may well have been contributing to the home while keeping little which could be counted as her own.

There is a discrepancy between the press reports of the reason for Miss Eamonson being unable to appear in court. The *Examiner* states that she was too ill to attend, while the *Chronicle* said that it was 'owing to the illness of an assistant'. Either way, she had employed Miss Anna Munro of the WFL National Executive to appear for

6   It was reported a week later that the *Chronicle* offices and other businesses had posters of a threatening nature pasted over their window and doors. What was said on them is not reported, so we cannot know which group may have been responsible.

her. The case against her was that she had been seen by PC Wilcox near Bayshill Terrace and he was suspicious as she was carrying a bag and he thought she might be a suffragette! He then found a placard on a pillar box in St George's Road and saw her fix to another on the other side of the road. Like Miss Boult and Miss Bales, she was taken to the police station and interviewed by Inspector Corbett. Miss Munro's defence was that the WFL did not recognise courts of law as women were not regarded as citizens, and that Miss Eamonson was acting on the instructions of the Executive of the WFL and therefore should not be prosecuted personally. She therefore pleaded not guilty, which was a rather strange difference from the other two – was there some difference of opinion between them on how to handle the case? The verdict and fine were the same for her as for the other two.

Presumably both Miss Boult and Miss Eamonson either paid the fine or had some of their property distrained, as they were both independent women of moderate means. But Miss Agnes Bales appears as a prisoner in the Roll of Honour of Suffragette Prisoners in the Suffragette Fellowship archive, which was put together in about 1950, from memory and personal testimony. She must have had to serve the fourteen days' imprisonment. Again, there are no local references, so this cannot be verified, but it seems that Cheltenham had its second suffragette prisoner![7]

---

7 Agnes Bales died in 1939 in Norfolk, where she and her parents had been born. In 1933, she was left the considerable sum of £1,200 by a wealthy member of Cheltenham's theosophy circle and subsequently moved from her house in Whaddon Road. Ruth Eamonson died in 1959 in Cheltenham, so it is possible that she provided the information to the Suffragette Fellowship, although Mrs Earengey was also still alive and her sister Edith How Martyn was very much involved in setting up the Fellowship in 1926.

THE SUFFRAGETTES AND THE CHELTENHAM BY-ELECTION

In early 1911, Miss Ada Flatman, a paid organiser for the WSPU, was sent from Liverpool to Cheltenham. As there are no WSPU records to give detailed accounts or minutes of decision-making, there is little to suggest why this was done. It was a time of curious ambivalence in WSPU policy. In November 1910, Asquith announced that there would be no more time for the Conciliation Bill (to grant the vote to about 1 million women). 'Black Friday' was the result. This was the notorious day when women protesters were subjected to police brutality and sexual harassment, so gaining the government adverse publicity. After Asquith's apparent promise to give time for another bill, a promise which Christabel Pankhurst thought insufficient, the 'Battle of Downing Street' ensued. The police were taken unawares

Miss Ada Flatman, the WSPU organiser, speaking in the Cheltenham by-election. (*Cheltenham Chronicle and Gloucestershire Graphic*, 29 April 1911)

and seventy-five women were convicted of window-breaking and other similar offences. There was a lull in action during the general election of December, as the WSPU hoped that there would be firmer commitment to a bill in the King's Speech in February 1911. When this did not happen, there was much disillusionment, but internal friction meant there was no clear policy of militancy.

Why did WSPU send an organiser to Cheltenham?

It is known that Ada Flatman had been pressing headquarters for a change of venue. She had been in Liverpool since 1909 but, in spite of being judged successful in her campaigns, had become disillusioned and spent eight months in correspondence with Mrs Pethick-Lawrence attempting to secure a move, apparently to London. The reason for her discontent is illuminating. After a successful first year building on the pre-existing membership with poster parades, selling *Votes for Women* on the street and the long Merseyside tradition of open-air meetings, she put herself at odds with the membership. She tried to get ladies to open their drawing-rooms during the winter in order for meetings to be held. This was unsuccessful, as the activists were not from the 'drawing-room' class, so she moved her attention to the Wirral where there were more wealthy recruits. An air of exclusivity developed which did not suit the Liverpool activists. They were not comfortable with meetings in drawing-rooms, cafes and tea-rooms and so tensions arose. It was apparent that Ada Flatman preferred a campaign with perhaps a more 'genteel' aura.[1]

Finally, Mrs Pethick-Lawrence wrote on 14 December 1910 (SF Archive):

I feel with you there is much to be said for a change. After a while one get (sic) to feel that one has given out all oneself and that a new public is necessary, and perhaps a new organiser will give another point of view and fresh inspiration to the old band of workers and members.

I think you will be pleased with the suggestion that Miss Pankhurst and I have to make to you. We have fallen in with your wishes to go to a new place to found a new centre.

But why did headquarters choose Cheltenham? It had a history of activity but not of radical militancy, and the short-lived WSPU had died. It was true that there was

---

1   K. Cowman: 'Mrs. Brown is a Friend and a Brother.'

an active WFL but, as Mrs Earengey had been co-operating with the WSS, it was unlikely that she would bring her small band of members over to the WSPU.

Were there any local WSPU members who had made overtures to headquarters? Again, this is impossible to know. There are brief annual reports remaining that give some details of subscriptions/donations and we can therefore see who in Cheltenham was supporting the union. Mrs Swiney gave money from 1907 to 1908, with sums of 2s 6d and 5s respectively, but she was so much the focus of Cheltenham WSS that she would not have wanted to encourage the formation of a strong WSPU in the town. Similarly, Mrs Earengey gave £2 in each of these two years but we know that her WSPU ties were only brief. The only other women listed before Miss Flatman's arrival are Mrs Jessie Pollock (who was another named supporter of the WSS, like Mrs Swiney) and Mrs Ann Selous, who gave £3 in 1907–08. Mrs Selous was the wife of Edmund Selous, who was a retired barrister/ornithologist, and they lived at 19 Clarence Square from 1901–07 (see Pittville History Works website). She appeared on local WSS platforms in this period but had moved away from the town.

Could Miss Flatman herself have requested Cheltenham? The wording of Mrs Pethick-Lawrence's letter above does not suggest that. Ada Flatman had briefly helped with the WSPU shop in Bristol, and then in Birmingham before going to Liverpool, but no closer connection has been found. It is, however, likely that she welcomed the choice. Although she was undoubtedly radical and driven by 'causes', she had some social pretensions which were satisfied through the WSPU as her time on Merseyside had proved.[2] Cheltenham society would have held a number of attractions for her.

Who was Ada Flatman?

Some detail of her life may reveal why this was so. Susan Ada Flatman was born in Littleport, Cambridgeshire, in 1871 into a fairly modest family.[3] Her father was a 'general dealer', variously described as a seedsman in church and other records,

---

2   She also brought with her to Cheltenham the local secretary from Liverpool, Geraldine Lyster, a young woman in her thirties who came from a very comfortable home in the more prestigious part of Liverpool. Her father had been a surgeon but died when she was young.

3   A baby given the identical name was born, baptised and died the previous year – it was not an unusual practice to give the next baby the same names.

and an agricultural labourer before his marriage, but something caused the family to move to Ealing, perhaps the failure of her father's business or a rift: in 1881, her father was described as a seed merchant lodging at a pub in Littleport, but her mother and five children were in Ealing, the two older brothers employed as a plasterer and grocer respectively. One of her other sisters, Marion Georgiana, was in service with a silversmith's family in Ealing too. Her father George died in Ealing in 1884, so he must have joined them, but the family did not prosper. In 1891, Ada and her sisters Annie and Alice were still with their mother in Ealing and all three young women were dressmakers. In 1901, there was a little more security as Ada and her mother were living with Alice and her husband in Fulham. He was a house decorator and sanitary engineer and was doing well enough to have one domestic servant – but Ada was still only a 'skirtfitter'. Two of her sisters 'married well' – Annie married an accountant in 1898 and Lufina, previously a lady's maid in Reigate, also married an accountant. It is therefore understandable that Ada had some social aspirations.

Ada's mother died in 1904. It was perhaps then that she made a foray into the wider world, because her reminiscences (which *do not* include her life before 1905) describe how in 1905 she met an Australian lady who lived at her club, who suggested she went to Sydney with her (SF Archive). Perhaps Ada was by then a member of some small ladies' club in London. Ladies' clubs had become something of a phenomenon in the latter years of the nineteenth century and some catered for lower middle-class and working women, while others had more in common with exclusive gentlemen's clubs. Ada Flatman's family history does not suggest she could have afforded high fees but her finances are a mystery, as she never hints at having had an occupation in these years. I doubt how far she was 'of independent means', although she would have earned a respectable living if she managed to get enough clients for her dressmaking and skirtfitting.

A Miss S.A. Flatman went to New York in 1904 as a 'governess' and returned in May 1905 with no occupation. It is hard to believe there was more than one with this name, and the dates fit in with the period after her mother's death. A spirit of wanderlust was to colour most of her life from then on, and speaks of wide horizons and a courageous spirit. She did not go to Australia until November 1906 according to passenger lists, and returned in 1907. In her reminiscences she describes several happy months in Australia and a return journey which she broke in Ceylon to visit a friend she had made on the outward journey, whose brother was a tea planter. Here she said she was introduced as 'their Suffragette friend', 'which I promptly repudiated'. When in Australia, she said that most women were interested in the British movement but she 'did not know anything of politics or social services' but knew of two young women imprisoned after an incident at the Free Trade Hall,

Manchester. This was in October 1905 when she was still in England, but one wonders why she should have been introduced as a suffragette in Ceylon if she had showed no interest in women's suffrage. However, her memories were written in 1946/7, so much could have been confused or the result of wishful thinking (Reminiscences in SF Archive).

She claimed that, on her return, she was determined to find out more and that she was not impressed by the suffragists, but was impressed by Christabel Pankhurst's speech at the Royal Horticultural Hall. She volunteered to take part in the deputation to Asquith in 1908 and, as a result, was imprisoned in Holloway for a month, an experience that she relished in hindsight because she felt part of something exciting and because of her proximity to Mrs Pankhurst. She does not describe how she was recruited as an organiser.[4]

The beginning of the WSPU campaign – eminent speakers

On her arrival in the town, Miss Flatman managed to get a positive *Looker-On* report with her photograph. The tone had been set, as this paper was very much aimed at the 'social set' in Cheltenham. It was announced that she had come from a hugely successful campaign in Liverpool and Cheshire and had come to 'open' the district:

> Mrs Pankhurst visits Cheltenham for the first time on Wednesday, February 15th, when she is speaking in the Town Hall. Following this meeting, Miss Flatman proposes to hold fortnightly 'At Homes' every first and third Tuesday in each month, both afternoon and evening, in the Town Hall, for which she has secured the help of prominent writers, actresses, and many other notable speakers …

The literary and artistic

This was an ambitious programme promising the kind of headline speakers who would attract audiences to the Town Hall. A letter from Beatrice Harraden dated 22 January attests to her speedy attempt to lure prestigious speakers to the town.

---

4 The 1946 BBC archive account by Miss Flatman of her own experiences gives a fascinating insight into her activities, but may not be entirely accurate!

Beatrice Harraden was a novelist and writer who had become an ardent suffragette. In many ways quiet and retiring, she suffered from ill health all her life, yet was prepared to appear on women's suffrage platforms. She had been recruited by the Actresses' Franchise League to write for the women's suffrage theatre and had written *Lady Geraldine's Speech*. Her letter to Miss Flatman said, 'I will come to Cheltenham (I was an old Cheltenham College girl) if it will do for me to read *Lady Geraldine's Speech*. I have no time to write anything new and you know that I am not a political speaker' (SF Archive).

Another letter from her in March reveals that her mother had just died, so she postponed her visit until May. When she did come to Cheltenham, she read her play at two meetings, and also gave some personal insight. She revealed that she supported the militant movement because her 'heart had gone out to the brave women struggling against such tremendous odds' (*Looker-On* 20/05/11). Touchingly, she also said that she was renewing her acquaintance with the town after being at Cheltenham Ladies' College under Miss Beale, but said she would never have come back if it had not been for the WSPU because of 'other associations of a painful nature – the death of Miss Beale for instance'. As this happened five years earlier, this is perhaps artistic hyperbole or a reaction to her mother's death. The play is very short and starts from an anti-suffrage position: Lady Geraldine has

Beatrice Harraden, writer and novelist, old girl of Cheltenham Ladies' College, who spoke for the WSPU in Cheltenham. (Wikipedia, George Grantham Bain Collection at US Library of Congress)

115

to make a speech but, in the course of preparing it with the help of her old school chum from her Cheltenham years, she is converted! The Cheltenham association would have attracted her audience.

Other notable names announced for the future included Lady Stout, Lady Constance Lytton, Miss Evelyn Sharp, the novelist, and Miss Decima Moore, 'a leading light of the stage' (*Looker-On* 18/02/11). The list of titled ladies and 'artistic' figures seems calculated to appeal to Cheltenham society. Miss Evelyn Sharp was a children's writer and talented journalist, often writing for the *Manchester Guardian*, who had been converted to the 'cause' in the early years of the WSPU. She had overcome her initial terror of public speaking to become one of their best speakers according to Mrs Pankhurst. When she addressed meetings in the Town Hall in March, she vehemently rejected the image of the militant woman as the kind of woman 'who wanted to shriek, to make a sensation or to draw attention to herself' (*Looker-On* 25/03/11). This was the image some of the press was peddling. She insisted that imprisonment would not crush their spirit – interesting as she had not yet been imprisoned, because her mother had made her promise not to do anything to cause this to happen. However, only four days after her speech in Cheltenham, her mother wrote a very moving letter absolving her from the promise and, by November, she was in prison for window-breaking!

Another of the speakers announced was Miss Decima Moore, the actress. She was a star of the theatre and of light opera (with the D'Oyly Carte Company) and was a prominent member of the Actresses' Franchise League (AFL). Her

Evelyn Sharp, writer and journalist, being arrested for being part of a deputation to the Home Secretary to discuss the 'Cat and Mouse' Act. She came to Cheltenham for the WSPU in 1911. (*Daily Mail*, 24 August 1913)

Decima Moore, actress, who declined to speak for the WSPU in Cheltenham but gave advice on good lodgings for visiting speakers! (Postcard in author's collection)

marriage to a senior army figure in 1905 which made her Lady Moore-Guggisberg would undoubtedly have made her even more acceptable in Cheltenham, in spite of the fact that she had divorced her first husband for adultery and cruelty, still a process which caused disapproval. Her frequent tours abroad with her husband, and correspondence kept by Ada Flatman, show that she could not fit in a visit to the town. Nevertheless, she provided information from her times performing in Cheltenham – she recommended to visiting campaigners 'theatrical rooms and used to serving meals at all times' run by Miss Coles at Nash Cottage for 20*s* for three rooms and bath (presumably for a week).[5] More importantly, she thought that Miss Flatman would 'have a pretty hard job' in getting support in the town (undated letter in SF Archive).

It is interesting that Miss Flatman either did not know about another actress's association with the town or did not consider her a worthy speaker. Lillah McCarthy was brought up in Cheltenham, starting life in 1875 at 383 High Street where her father, Jonadab, was a dealer in works of art. Subsequently (1881 and 1891 censuses) they were living in Hartley House, Albion Street. In 1893 the family left for London and she began a highly successful acting career in which she played for some of the most illustrious managers and playwrights, including George Bernard Shaw. She also joined the AFL and one of her performances was for the WFL Old World Fair at the Caxton Hall, London, where a 'star cast' played *How the Vote was Won*.[6]

---

5   The Nash Cottages were in St Margaret's Road, I think, and were let/run by the Coles family. If Decima Moore really meant 'Miss', that would be Florence (33) or Alice (25) who was an artist.

6   This play by Cicely Hamilton and Christopher St John was probably the most well-known of the propaganda plays which were produced for the AFL.

Lillah McCarthy, Cheltenham-born actress, who was involved in the WSPU and the Actresses' Franchise League. (Postcard in author's collection)

Lillah McCarthy claimed to have been the AFL treasurer for a short period before being rescued from shame of mismanagement by Mr Pethick-Lawrence of the WSPU. She also claimed to have walked in WSPU processions and 'carried banners for Mrs Pankhurst and the Cause' (Lillah McCarthy: *Myself and My Friends*, p. 148). Her suffragette stance did not seem to have affected the close friendship she claimed with Asquith. In the somewhat overblown style of her autobiography, *Myself and My Friends*, she claimed that when visiting 10 Downing Street for a rehearsal for playing in front of the king and queen, she found herself alone in the Cabinet Room!

There were the baskets of papers and there was the blotting pad with its large sheet of immaculate white blotting paper, the austere solid ornaments of the Prime Minister's desk. I felt like a Joan of Arc of the ballot-box. Martyrdom or not, the occasion must be seized. I opened my box of grease paints, tool out the reddest stick I could find, and wrote across the blotting paper 'Votes for Women'. I went out of the room exultant.

After this apparent coup, she maintains that Asquith gave her the opportunity to explain her views on women's suffrage. However, by her own admission, she made 'a greater mess of public speaking for, without the footlights to protect me, I was lost' so was not a candidate for Miss Flatman's list of speakers.

The socially acceptable

Miss Flatman's attempts to appeal to the respectable and wealthier sections of Cheltenham society can be seen not only in the speakers invited, but also in the pattern of the meetings. The Town Hall 'At Homes' were held in the afternoon and the evening. The 3 p.m. meeting was by invitation only, the 8 p.m. meeting was open to the general public, but a silver collection was to be taken at both times. This was not calculated to draw in the lower classes: there were parts of the country where the WSPU concentrated on attracting the working classes, but many felt that the Pankhursts were more interested in wealthier women.

The *Looker-On* (03/03/11) reported that the audience to hear Lady Constance Lytton in an afternoon meeting in March was a 'large and fashionable gathering' presided over by the Rector of Cheltenham, Rev. l'Estrange Fawcett (11 March). Lady Constance carried a particular social cache. She was the daughter of the Viceroy of India during the 1870s, so some of the older Cheltenham ex-colonials would have served under him. However, she also had become famous in her own right for her WSPU work. By the time she visited Cheltenham, she had been imprisoned three times but had attracted most attention because, after realising that her title had given her special treatment on both the first two occasions, she disguised herself as a London seamstress, Jane Warton, when demonstrating outside Walton Gaol, Liverpool. While imprisoned, she went on hunger strike (in spite of suffering from a heart weakness) and it took a while for the prison staff to realise that she was not who she claimed to be. So she experienced the harsh treatment that she was then able to publicise in the suffrage press and in *The Times*: she was force-fed eight times in a very brutal fashion.

Lady Lytton spoke to the evening meeting of some of her gaol experiences, whereas she appears to have been less graphic in the genteel afternoon one. But she did not hesitate to say that she had not come to apologise for being a 'hooligan' but to tell them about the greatness of the movement of which she was a part. Where women fulfilled the same qualifications as men, they should be given the vote. The evening meeting, chaired by Miss Flatman, emphasised the need to protect the interests of working women: whether many were present is doubtful.

Lady Constance Lytton and Annie Kenney having planted a tree in the Suffragette
'Arboretum' at the home of the Blathwayts, Batheaston, Somerset, in April 1909. Both
women spoke in the Cheltenham and Cotswold area in 1911 and 1912.
(© Bath inTime)

The biggest attraction was the arrival of Mrs Pankhurst for a meeting on
15 February. This was seen as a launch-pad for the WSPU in the town, as it was
their first public meeting. It was not public in the sense of its being free, with the
seats priced at 2s 6d, 1s, and 6d. Miss Flatman opened proceedings by saying that
she knew there was a strong body of 'Antis' in the town but that she hoped they
would have their eyes opened, especially to the moral aspect of the question. Mrs
Pankhurst also mused as to whether there were opponents in the audience[7] but
she was keen to point out how many women in the town who were ratepayers
and rentpayers, householders and lodgers, should be interested in the cause. Just as
women had to fight to prove themselves in education and in certain 'avenues of

7   There were no recorded incidences of dissent – and she was frequently applauded.

120

employment', so they needed to fight for the right to vote. She spoke of it as a civil war, with women moved by the same spirit that had led the barons to take up the sword against King John! Military terminology was frequently used by the WSPU leaders and perhaps would have resonated with many members of the audience. She was prepared to use this local association to persuade her audience:

> Five thousand British men lost their lives during the two years of the South African War, and in the same period ten thousand women gave their lives in bringing life into the world. The women went to a lonely battlefield of their own, more terrible to face than that on which there were comradeship and bands of music.
>
> (*Examiner* 16/02/11)

Questioned about her views on the census being taken in two months' time, she declared that she intended to throw her paper in the fire as, until she was treated as a human being, she was not prepared to help the government. As has been seen, the WSPU was declaring its position on this in the same way as the WFL. One other question reveals potential hostility and some class concern. Someone asked whether the lodgers to be enfranchised would include 'an undesirable class of women': she replied 'Yes, and the lodgers now enfranchised include undesirable men.' As some of Cheltenham's teachers, and even women of private means, were lodgers, the question and answer might not have attracted universal agreement!

One amusing result of Mrs Pankhurst's visit was a somewhat ironic letter to the *Echo* from a father lamenting the effect of the meeting on his daughters. They had returned enthused by the cause and now wanted to emulate Sylvia Pankhurst, and also be an MP:

> Unfortunately, my daughters have not enough talent to make any fame out of literature or the arts, and they are convinced that the quickest, cheapest, and easiest way to gain notoriety is to become a militant suffragette. They used to attend to their house duties in a calm and methodical manner; now their attitude is a desire to assault everything.

A less amusing follow-up letter from 'Another Father' accused the women of untruths, hysteria and of showing what will happen if women were allowed into politics! Ada Flatman's rejoinder to the first letter tried to replicate his wry humour but, in the end, could only accuse him of 'writing such fictitious drivel to the Press' (*Echo* 02/03/11).

The by-election campaign

Although much of the speakers' emphasis was on the coming census, there was soon another reason for increased activity and heightened tension. In the general election of December 1910, the Liberal Richard Mathias defeated Viscount Duncannon, the Conservative sitting member. However, in January 1911, a petition was begun against Mathias for exceeding election expenses and abusing the rules – not exactly a case of gross corruption but a matter which the local Conservatives were prepared to pursue. The case dragged on until the end of March, and Mathias was then unseated and a new election was called with only four weeks for the campaigning.

All women's suffrage societies, but particularly the WSPU, welcomed a by-election because they could muster all their forces to one location and could publicise the views of each candidate on the one issue. In recent elections, the WSPU had campaigned vigorously against the Liberal candidates because their government was not seen to be sympathetic. As the Cheltenham election came later in the same month as the census, big names and forces added momentum to the local drive to establish a branch.

Cheltenham WSPU headquarters and shop in the High Street during the 1911 by-election. (*Gloucester Citizen*, 28 April 1911)

Miss Flatman thus had huge advantages in her mission. She swung into action with an appeal in *Votes for Women* (07/04/11) for help in shopkeeping, bill-distributing, paper-selling, speaking, chairing meetings, financial help or the use of a motor car. Committee rooms were set up at 64A High Street[8] and it was said that great interest was shown by passers-by as the premises were decorated with posters, etc. The window was tastefully dressed by Miss Stirling (one of the census evaders) with a huge 'Double-faced Asquith' displayed across it. The accounts in *VFW* are not very full and little remains in the Flatman archive relating to that period. However, *VFW* records that the Conservative candidate James Agg-Gardner was putting support for women's suffrage in his electoral address, while Major Mathias (the brother of the unseated MP) had sent to the Liberal Women's Federation a very unsatisfactory set of answers on the issue. There is a delightful report of somewhat farcical events, presumably submitted to the paper by Ada Flatman.

> Comic relief to the situation has been provided by Mrs Mathias (the unseated member's wife) and her children driving through the constituency in a motor-car holding a bannerette with the wording 'Vote for Daddy's Brother' and circling round and round the WSPU meetings, tooting their motor horn, while the Suffragists have had a little bannerette in green, on which, in purple lettering, 'I Don't Vote For Daddy's Brother, but for all his sisters, his cousins and his aunts, by keeping the Liberal out!'
>
> (*VFW* 28/04/11)

How far Ada Flatman was responsible for getting national figures to join the campaign is not known. Two letters survive from Mrs Pankhurst to her, which give some indication of what she felt about a visit. One, written from Ruthin, North Wales, on 13 April says that she cannot come 'next week' as she has had an urgent call to return to London. What seems to be perhaps the one before that, but is undated and from Carnarvon, says that she could come on the 18th and stay until the end of the election campaign, but 'I'm not much use for open air work but can take any number of indoor meetings in halls small or large. You know I attach great importance to women's afternoon meetings for you get results from them.' She went

---

8   The old numbering system started at 1 at the Hales Road end and went in single numbers along the north side until the Gloucester Road junction, so this would have been on the north side somewhere before the Promenade junction.

on to say that she did not think that only one meeting was much use (SF Archive). As she did not come in the end, it is difficult to know whether there was further correspondence and whether she was unable or unwilling to come.

What did arrive was the WSPU car, with Miss Vera Holme as the driver. This car was not the one in which Mrs Pankhurst was driven to Cirencester in July by Aileen Preston. It preceded that one and had been given to Mrs Pethick-Lawrence on her release from prison. She then gave it to the WSPU to use as an official car. It was an Austin, specially painted and upholstered in the colours of green, white and purple – with a narrow purple stripe lining the green body, white accented wheels and green and purple upholstery. The *Looker-On* describes the 'magnificent campaign in Cheltenham, where their motor-car, upholstered in the colours, and with flags flying in the well-known purple, white and green' (22/04/11). Vera Holme was the driver of whom Emmeline Pankhurst was a little suspicious, as she described her as 'giddy'. This was the result of her behaviour around the headquarters offices where she had a reputation for high spirits. Nicknamed 'Jacko' or 'Jack', she combined her

The 1911 Cheltenham by-election – the car in WSPU colours driven by Vera Holme (standing, left), also an actress and singer. Her driving skills were not always trusted by Mrs Pankhurst! (*Cheltenham Chronicle and Gloucestershire Graphic*, 29 April 1911)

work for the WSPU with continued work as an actress and singer. She had worked for the D'Oyly Carte Opera Company and was a member of the AFL.

Miss Flatman certainly mustered big names for the election campaign. These included Annie Kenney, the 'mill-girl' now the WSPU organiser in Bristol, Charlotte Marsh, a qualified sanitary inspector who had joined the WSPU after witnessing some terrible social conditions and was also to become an organiser,[9] and Georgina Brackenbury, an artist from a military family who was to become one of the WSPU's most effective speakers. Lady Stout, the wife of the ex-Prime Minister of New Zealand and now Lord Chief Justice, was one of those advertised earlier in the year. As a colonial lady of social importance who had seen the women's vote in operation, her presence was now even more relevant. She was able to tell her audience that she had possessed the vote for seventeen years and that neither she nor New Zealand had deteriorated as a result! In fact, women had been a good moral influence on male voters and she painted a picture of a country in the process of conquering most of the social ills such as infant mortality and drunkenness. She linked temperance reform to the women's vote, as women had told the premier that they were only prepared to support compulsory military training for their sons if alcohol was banned from the camps. Only brewers were against women's suffrage in New Zealand! Reports suggest the audience was enthusiastic (*Looker-On* 08/04/11, *Echo* 06/04/11).

Foremost among the speakers were Mrs Emmeline Pethick-Lawrence, the WSPU treasurer and joint editor of *VFW*, and Christabel Pankhurst. Mrs Pethick-Lawrence had already visited in March to great acclaim, but came back to lend a hand to the campaign. Using historical precedents such as Magna Carta and Simon de Montfort, she told Cheltenham that its by-election was about 'fundamental human liberty'. She pleaded for support for the Conciliation Bill which would enfranchise households headed by a woman 'from the duchess in her palace to the charwoman in her cottage' and would give 1 million women the vote. Although brought up as a Liberal, she could not support any party that did not recognise her as a woman. Miss Flatman's report to *VFW* said that the Town Hall was packed for the meeting with many having to be turned away, and that none of the expected Liberal interruptions occurred.

Surprisingly, it seems that Christabel Pankhurst's eve of poll meeting was not 'packed'. 'There was a large mixed audience' but not all the seating was occupied.

---

9   She was also one of the first two women to be forcibly fed in prison.

A parade in Cheltenham for Christabel Pankhurst's eve of poll meeting during the by-election campaign. (*Cheltenham Chronicle and Gloucestershire Graphic*, 29 April 1911)

Introduced as 'the young champion of the cause' by Miss Flatman,[10] Christabel tried to bring a unifying tone to the final day of the campaign by suggesting that women's suffrage was neither a class nor a party issue. She refuted the idea that women could not understand 'Imperial questions' with the somewhat dubious but crowd-pleasing examples of Queen Elizabeth and Queen Victoria. She appealed to the military background of some listeners by saying that the country needed the Florence Nightingales in war as much as they needed the Tommy Atkins. Introducing some wit, she said that Asquith needed a tonic, bitter to the taste but good for the constitution. And Cheltenham women could provide that tonic 'by putting on the screw. Fifty votes will turn the scale.' However moderate she tried to be, at the end she could not resist mentioning that women were prepared to go

10 She was 30 at the time.

Poster advertising open-air WSPU meetings during the 1911 Cheltenham by-election. Annie Kenney, the former mill-girl, was the star attraction. (Suffragette Fellowship Archive © Museum of London)

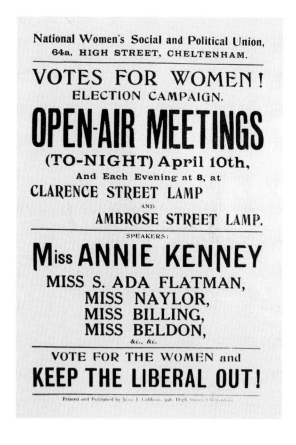

National Women's Social and Political Union,
64a, HIGH STREET, CHELTENHAM.

VOTES FOR WOMEN!
ELECTION CAMPAIGN.

OPEN-AIR MEETINGS
(TO-NIGHT) April 10th,
And Each Evening at 8, at
CLARENCE STREET LAMP
AND
AMBROSE STREET LAMP.

SPEAKERS:
Miss ANNIE KENNEY
MISS S. ADA FLATMAN,
MISS NAYLOR,
MISS BILLING,
MISS BELDON,
&c., &c.

VOTE FOR THE WOMEN and
KEEP THE LIBERAL OUT!

Printed and Published by Jesse J. Guilham, pub. High Street, Cheltenham.

to prison for the cause, to risk their lives for it and to suffer stigma for it (*Looker-On* 29/04/11, *VFW* 05/05/11).[11]

The campaign was not only conducted from the genteel surroundings of the Town Hall or the safety of King's Hall. Miss Flatman adopted the usual election pattern of street meetings by using venues such as the Clarence Street and Ambrose Street Lamps. These were much more exposed venues and organised gangs of youths, sometimes in Liberal colours, tried to break up the meetings and, on one occasion, prevented hundreds (sic) of people hearing Annie Kenney speak. Sometimes meetings were not advertised in order to avoid this happening (*VFW* 21/04/11). In addition, at least two meetings were held in the outer reaches of the constituency – at Charlton Kings.

---

11 All the noteworthy WSPU figures stayed at the Queen's Hotel just before the election.

The suggestion of organised Liberal opposition is well-founded, as the WSPU were running a campaign to 'Keep the Liberal Out'. This was the policy they had adopted nationally as long as the government refused to grant what they requested. While they did not overtly support the Cheltenham Conservative candidate, James Agg-Gardner, they did not oppose him and he had the added advantage of being consistently supportive of women's suffrage.

The result of the election could hardly have been closer. After six re-counts, it was declared that Agg-Gardner had won by just four votes. Miss Flatman had requested entry to the count but a surviving letter from the mayor, Charles Margrett, who had some sympathy with the cause, shows that this was not granted. However, he enclosed a ticket for the Lobby for her and two lady friends which 'will afford you the opportunity you desire speaking to the successful Candidate when he leaves the Counting Room' (Letter of 28 April – SF Archive). Why there is then a picture of her on the balcony with the unsuccessful Major Mathias after the declaration is a mystery. The WSPU could claim that they had swayed the result. The Winter Gardens behind the Town Hall showed pictures of the women's suffrage

Electors, these things are a national scandal. Will you put a stop to it now by making the Government give votes to women? Cost what it may, women will never give up the fight until the vote is won. Electors, it is your duty to lend a hand, and by voting against the Government to get votes for women before any further sacrifices have to be made.

Electors of Cheltenham, we call upon you to stand by the women who are fighting for their freedom. We ask you to get a pledge before polling day that women householders shall have the vote this year. If you do not get this pledge we call on you to mark your disapproval of the attitude of Mr. Asquith and his Government by

voting against Major Mathias.
VOTE AGAINST THE GOVERNMENT AND KEEP THE LIBERAL OUT.

Signed on behalf of the Women's Social and Political Union:—

APRIL, 1911.   E. PANKHURST.

Local Committee Rooms: 64A, HIGH STREET, CHELTENHAM.

Read "VOTES FOR WOMEN" Weekly, One Penny, from all Newsagents and Booksellers.

Printed and Published by THE WOMEN'S SOCIAL & POLITICAL UNION.

Detail from a WSPU poster explaining why and how they wanted to 'Keep the Liberal Out' in the 1911 Cheltenham by-election. WSPU tactics were aimed at defeating Liberal candidates as their government continued to refuse to accommodate any bill on women's suffrage. (Suffragette Fellowship Archive © Museum of London)

Miss Flatman, the WSPU organiser in Cheltenham, exchanging words on the balcony of the Town Hall with the defeated Liberal candidate in the 1911 by-election. (*Cheltenham Chronicle and Gloucestershire Graphic*, 6 May 1911)

campaigners during the election, and it was claimed that they were greeted by cheers (*VFW* 12/05/11). But there were other factors at work; Agg-Gardner was the 'local' candidate for example.

However, in an extensive section from other national reports in the *Echo*, it is only in the *Daily Mail* that the influence of women is even mentioned. The interpretation of its war correspondent was that, when the Liberals excluded women from their last Town Hall meeting, allegedly because of space, they alienated the younger women of Cheltenham. The reporter suggests that some Liberal women switched their allegiance and became entranced by the Conservative blue instead of the Liberal yellow. The Liberals' decision was contrasted with the Conservatives': they allowed women in to their final meeting and they filled the gallery and orchestra space. As a result, the Promenade was filled with ladies wearing blue, followed by a Liberal attempt to get working-class women out on to the streets in yellow (*Echo* 28/04/11). He assumes that the women would have had an influence over the male voters, but this was not attributable to WSPU activity.

8

Cheltenham WSPU: The Realities of Existence as a Branch

A new WSPU branch is formed

In the pages of *Votes for Women* in May 1911, it was announced that a new branch was to be formed to 'carry on the work'. The ferment of activity in the last few months had laid a basis and it was emphasised that every member should go to the meeting at the home of Mrs Reginald (Mrs C.) Fergus(s)on at Bedford Lodge, College Road. She became the first honorary secretary and in April had offered to provide free copies of the paper to the public library so that all suffragettes could read it. Her house was also used for meetings on a number of occasions and had been used on census night. She was the wife of Reginald John de Gale Ferguson who was a planter in Grenada. The first of their two daughters, Audrey, was born there shortly after their marriage but otherwise, Mrs Ferguson seems to have moved around between desirable places in England while her husband moved back and forth to Grenada. Although her origins were 'trade' (the daughter of a Lancashire general carrier and agent), she clearly had the social prestige in Cheltenham which would have satisfied Miss Flatman.

One gets the impression from the branch reports sent in to *Votes for Women* that it was a struggle to keep going and that, apart from gaining a few key speakers to the town, the group could easily be dragged into the minutiae of selling the paper and preparing goods for the WSPU Christmas Fair in London. The Gloucestershire branches were providing goods for the woollen stall and, as the time approached, began to hold working parties in Cheltenham, presumably all knitting vigorously! A shop was taken for a few days to sell leftover goods and there was even a 10s prize offered for the best knitted scarf – not quite what some women would have imagined they had joined the WSPU to do! What is sad is that the lack of branch minutes deprives us of a real insight into what went on: Miss Flatman's reports may have been calculated to show that she was doing the will of her political masters, but also reflect that her energies were rather dissipated as she was trying to organise Cheltenham, Cirencester, Stroud and Gloucester in this period.

The above is not an entirely fair representation of the branch's activities. There were visits from Beatrice Harraden (again), Georgina Brackenbury and in November from Mrs Pethick-Lawrence. The summer of 1911 was a time of hope for the women's movement as it appeared that the government had promised to grant time for a women's suffrage bill in 1912. Even Christabel Pankhurst appeared to believe this, and the WSPU did not automatically oppose Liberals at by-elections as in the past. The atmosphere was more muted and the biggest event was the Women's Coronation Procession, organised by all the suffrage societies in a spirit of co-operation: it took place on the Saturday before the coronation of George V and was a march along the length of the coronation route. We know from the pages of *VFW* that some Cheltenham WSPU women went to this remarkable event and were numbered among the 40,000 there. Carriages were reserved on the 11.15 train for 12*s* return, quite an expensive trip, but it was later suggested that there might be a cheaper excursion rate via Waterloo. Cheltenham women were told to find their banner between Cleopatra's Needle and Waterloo Bridge. Sadly, we have no record of this banner but know that it adorned the Cheltenham box at the Albert Hall at the end of the march, and was later presented to the branch by Miss E.L. Andrews, of whom more later.[1]

As 1911 came to a close, the optimistic mood of the WSPU, led by Christabel while her mother was touring the USA, changed to one of anger. Although Asquith did not entirely renege on his previous promise, he now announced that he would introduce a bill to extend the men's vote to the 4 million still excluded and would consider an amendment on women's suffrage. This was potentially more democratic but robbed the women of their own bill. The WSPU therefore called off their truce and organised a deputation to Asquith. The local secretary, presumably still Mrs Ferguson, asked for names to be put forward, but we do not know whether any responded. While the movement now erupted into more violence with window-

---

1   *VFW* also records that Miss Winifred Boult of Cheltenham was organising the national Gymnastic Teachers' Suffrage Society participation in the procession. She specified that women should wear a white shirt, white tie and short navy skirt with no hat. 'Uniformity of appearance and good marching must be the keynote' (09/06/11).

smashing and setting fire to pillar boxes, the Cheltenham society continued in a low-key manner – but still seemed to have retained its membership, in spite of attacks on national tactics by the local press and by their MP Agg-Gardner.

It seems that in 1912 the members concentrated on selling *VFW*, not only in the street, which often led to women being abused or threatened, but also door-to-door. Members' meetings, often advertised as drawing-room meetings, were held in various homes, although we know of one open-air meeting at the Clarence Street Lamp in May. It was reported that there was a large and interested audience and all copies of *VFW* were sold. This pattern was repeated when Mrs Flora Drummond visited. Known as 'The General', this stout fiery Scots lady who had trained as a typist became a leading WSPU figure and had headed the procession in June mounted on a horse. It was reported that Mrs Drummond gave a most inspiring and helpful address in the home of the local president. Her speech at the lamp 'was heckled pretty frequently, but she was listened to with close attention when she made an appeal for the enfranchisement of women as a

Mrs (General) Flora Drummond before leading a suffragette procession in London, 1909. (www.wikitree. com/photo/jpg/Gibson-5654-1)

means for putting a stop to the white slave traffic and raising the moral standard of the nation' (*Echo* 04/05/12).

The pattern of money-raising continued into 1913, with a jumble sale at Bayshill Lecture Hall, sales of home-made sweets and fortnightly members' meetings. The first public meeting for many months was in the large drawing-room of the Town Hall in February when Miss Kathleen Jarvis gave a 'splendid fighting speech' (*VFW* 28/02/13). Kathleen Jarvis was not one of the most prominent WSPU speakers and it is significant that the report (*Suffragette* 28/02/13) makes more of the speech by Dr Alice Burn, now based in Cheltenham, who was able to relate her experience as a voter in New Zealand.[2] She was to play an increasingly active part in the town and may have been trying to wake it from its sleepiness, which contrasted with what was happening nationally. Urgent pleas for attendance of members at meetings are coupled with the perennial working parties for the Christmas Sale and a jumble sale. A reference to 5*s* being contributed to the Emily Davison Funeral Expenses Fund shows that there was some awareness of the bigger national picture: Emily Davison had died after running out in front of the king's horse at the Epsom Derby. But 5*s* was not much in the grand scheme of jumble sales and woollen goods!

Part of the attempt to reawaken Cheltenham may have been the appearance of the Men's Political Union in the town. Although some of the MPU leaders were concerned about WSPU violence, they did co-operate with local branches such as Cheltenham. Mr Gillespie, the head of the national body, spoke at a meeting chaired by Alice Burn, and Mr J.F. Caudle then agreed to form a branch. Mr Caudle had been active in the ILP and was a checker in a bootmaking business. He lived in Hall Road, Leckhampton, in 1911 and, although he was in the *upper* working class, he came from a different social sphere from most of the local WSPU committee members. When Mr Gillespie visited a second time, there was an appeal to the WSPU for paper-sellers. The chair was taken by the new secretary, Miss Andrews, and Mr Gillespie addressed a small gathering in fiery tones, advocating rebellion against unjust laws and placing himself very firmly on the left of politics. Again, this might have made some of the WSPU members uncomfortable.

---

2   See chapter 5 for more on Dr Burn's career and beliefs.

Cheltenham Ladies' College and the WSPU

As has been pointed out, no branch records remain and, for security reasons, the WSPU did not keep a membership roll, so fragments of information have to be gleaned from local newspaper and suffrage press reports. We do know who filled the role of honorary secretary in this period. Mrs Constance Ferguson of College Road was the first and her background is described at the beginning of the chapter. In early 1912 the new secretary was Mrs W.L. Mellersh of Bergholt, Painswick Road, who had evaded the 1911 census. However, her tenure was brief and in April, Miss E.L. Andrews of 2 Vittoria Walk took over. She had already been active during the previous year, helping with publicity for meetings and hosting a meeting at her home.

Miss Ellen Louise Andrews is a significant figure because she was a teacher at Cheltenham Ladies' College. It has often (wrongly) been assumed that the school was a hotbed of suffrage activism. It certainly inculcated feminist ideas in girls and gave them aspirations they might otherwise not have had. However, the suffragist principal Miss Beale had died before the extent of WSPU militancy had been realised, and her successor, Miss Faithfull, was clear that her staff remained objective in their views. There had been reports that 300 girls took part in a suffrage procession. In a letter to *The Times* (18/04/12), she denied that this was so. She also took pains to argue that:

> a teacher may hold very strong partisan views and yet feel in honour bound not to influence her pupils … To stifle discussion of the suffrage question among girls would be to stimulate interest in it, but to use the authority of a teacher in directing their views on the subject would be to my mind indefensible. In our body of over 100 teachers there is, I am convinced, the most loyal observance of the unwritten law that there should be no proselytizing.

However, Miss Andrews did take up an official position with the WSPU before she retired in July 1912, and her sister Miss Alice Andrews took the chair at a meeting in the Town Hall in June 1911: like her sister, she was a highly respected teacher, a close friend of Miss Beale and retired in July 1912. So the sisters were publicly supporting the militant wing of the movement while still teaching, Miss E.L. (Nellie) as head of the junior school and a German teacher, and Miss Alice in

---

3   When Alice died in 1944 the Guild Leaflet tribute recalled her as the last outstanding member of Miss Beale's day. 'Not a brilliant woman herself, she disciplined and helped to mature many brains finer than her own, and her reward came in their success.'

Miss Alice Andrews, teacher at Cheltenham Ladies' College, with the then headmistress, Dorothea Beale. Miss Andrews supported the WSPU and meetings were held in their house when her sister, Ellen, was local secretary from 1912. (F. Cecily Steadman: *In the Days of Miss Beale, London and Cheltenham,* 1931)

charge of the Cambridge Room.[3] Many meetings and working parties were held at their home in Vittoria Walk, albeit primarily after their retirement from teaching. Their oldest sister Constance had retired as a CLC teacher in 1907, but she also supported the cause with a signature under the WFL/CUWFA groups in 1912.[4]

How many other staff were involved? Was Miss Faithfull's letter accurate? Only two teachers have emerged as overt activists: both claimed a parliamentary vote in the test case of 1909 with WSS and WFL figures like Mrs Mills and Misses Boult and Eamonson. This was a very public step to take. M'elle Berthe Murciani of Sans Souci, St Luke's, was a teacher of languages and Madame Anne von Elischer of 4 Orrisdale Terrace, a widow, taught music. They do not appear in other reports except that Mme Elischer entertained at a WSS Garden Fair.[5]

We do not know of any other active participants, but the dusty 1912 book in the Gloucestershire Archives, together with the 1911 census, reveals the identities of other

---

4   All three sisters had been pupils at the school and had been among the first to take public exams there. They then were immediately employed as teachers, presumably training under Miss Beale's excellent 'in-house' scheme.

5   Her employment at CLC ended in 1911 so she may have left the town then. M'elle Murciani remained a teacher until 1918.

supporters. A little group of young teachers in their twenties or early thirties signed as 'Sympathisers', possibly completely unaligned, or perhaps supporters of the WSPU as there was not an official section for them. Obituaries in the Guild Magazines give an insight into the characters of these women and they seem to fit with radical sympathies. Millicent Taylor lived for a while in Horsefair Street, Charlton Kings, and taught chemistry: she was an ex-pupil, an amazing young woman who, after gaining her BSc, wanted to gain her doctorate and cycled back and forth to Bristol at weekends to achieve this! Philippa Drew lived in Suffolk Square and had a similarly colourful life. She had been studying to become a concert pianist until an accident damaged her hands. She taught geography, maths and German. But it is her cycling (the length of Norway to Finland) and climbing alone in Europe at a time when such behaviour was not the norm for a woman that indicates her tremendous spirit, what is called 'her fire undimmed' in her obituary. Others in this group included Edith Fergusson who taught the younger girls and lived with her family, some of whom were CUWFA members, at St Philip's Lodge in Painswick Road. She battled ill health for many years. Charlotte Houston was in Astell boarding house and taught languages and Agnes Rosseter, a Froebel-trained teacher, was in Lansdown Place boarding house. Interestingly, a contribution to WSPU funds of the considerable sum of 4s 6d was given by Dorothea Rangeley Hensley, a 16-year-old part-time American student.

Signing as members of the Conservative and Unionist Women's Franchise Association were three boarding house staff – Miss Georgiana Lacy, Miss Marian Allen and Miss Lucy Herbert. Miss Lacy had retired from running a boarding house, Hollym, in Parabola Road in 1911. She was another woman of tremendous courage and enterprise who had come to Cheltenham in her thirties to try to make a living. She set up an independent boarding house used by college students but always had 'the confidence of Miss Beale' and kept in close touch with the teachers of her boarders. Miss Allen was head of the boarding house Glengar for twenty-five years and Miss Herbert, an ex-pupil, became her secretary and companion. Miss Constance Cooke, the last of the housemistresses appointed by Miss Beale, was a member of the WSS. She was an ex-pupil, Oxford graduate, and ran the section of the college for senior students who were either working for external degrees or training to teach. As someone who 'could not bear the second-rate or the crooked', one can imagine her as forthright in her opinions.[6]

---

6   Information from guild magazines of 1961 and 1968, guild leaflets of 1921, 1934 and 1965. Also 1951 college magazine.

Miss Elizabeth Guinness,
Vice Principal of Cheltenham
Ladies' College, who in 1913
stood as an independent
candidate for the local council.
Her campaign was dogged
by attackers claiming that
she was a suffragette – she
was not, but supported the
suffragists. (*Cheltenham Chronicle
and Gloucestershire Graphic*,
11 October 1913)

One CLC lady made more of a mark in the town but she was not a fervent activist as her opponents alleged. Miss Elizabeth Guinness, vice principal from 1908 to 1924, had signed the public book of support as a WSS member in 1912 and the following year stood as an independent candidate for Middle Ward in the town council elections. She did so with the support of Miss Faithfull, the principal, and of Dr Earengey, whose women's suffrage credentials were well known. Her election address anticipated the attacks she would encounter by stating: 'Although the question of Women's Suffrage is here irrelevant, to correct misrepresentation I wish to add that I deplore and detest the recent actions of the Suffragettes' (*Looker-On* 18/10/13). She was unsuccessful, but to put herself in the public domain in this way was very courageous in light of the many attacks made on her – questioning her 'Radicalism', her ability to do the job and her attempt to introduce 'petticoat government'![7]

7   Elizabeth Guinness was the daughter of the Vicar of Banbury. She had an Oxford degree and had previously lectured in English and been vice principal at Royal Holloway College.

Who else supported the WSPU?

Officials of the branch who are mentioned in *VFW* reports can be identified, and suggest that the genteel image which Miss Flatman seemed to crave had been continued. The treasurer from 1912 was Mrs Alice Hill of Charlton Kings, who was the newly married young wife of a retired coffee planter.[8] Miss Annie Gooding gave some secretarial help to the branch: she was the middle-aged daughter of a retired doctor and lived in a large house in Lypiatt Road. The chair of a public meeting in 1911 was Miss Margaret Gardiner, who was a retired schoolmistress and lived with her brother Charles, also a schoolmaster, in Paragon Parade, tended to by two domestic servants. (He had recently married a CLC teacher of music – see Census Evasion section.) In the absence of the first secretary Mrs Ferguson, Miss Gertrude Blandford of St George's Parade took over. She was a working woman rather than one who could survive on independent means, being a buyer for a draper in the town, not quite part of Miss Flatman's collection of 'ladies'. Her willingness to sell the paper at an anti-suffrage meeting in 1911 says much about her practical attitude to being a suffragette. Another lady from the drapery world was a Miss Ralph of Cavendish House, who took over as treasurer in 1914. Also very practical but from a more comfortable background was Miss Eira Wheeler of Middleton Lodge, St George's Road, who was the young daughter of a solicitor's widow. She was saddled with the role of secretary of the Fete Society and it was to her that the woollen goods had to be given! She was probably relieved of 'woollen' responsibility to be married the next year in a big society wedding, but this may have snuffed out her militancy.[9]

It is easy to distort what the membership was like from such fragmentary information. There are WSPU annual reports of donations and they are usually in geographical groups or under the name of the organiser in the pages of *VFW*, so enabling us to identify a few local women who were prepared and able to donate. However, some women who were members of other societies gave money in sympathy with the treatment that the militants received: in Cheltenham, this

---

8   Before her marriage she was a teacher of cookery, but it is unknown where she taught. She certainly seems to have married 'up'.

9   An interesting aside on this story is that the *Stroud News* gave an extensive wedding present list. The social network from which so many of the women's suffrage supporters came is shown in gifts from the Swineys of the WSS, Lieutenant-Colonel Ashburner (WSS), l'Estrange Fawcetts (CUWFA), Mrs Seaforth Mackenzie (WSS), Major and Mrs Brooke-Murray (CUWFA) and Miss E.L. Andrews (WSPU).

The marriage of Miss Eira Wheeler, Cheltenham WSPU activist, to a Stroud clergyman. Her activities appear to have ended after her marriage. (*Stroud Journal*, 21 June 1912)

included figures such as Mrs Swiney in early years. In 1911, *VFW* recorded forty-seven donations to the Self-Denial Fund[10] collected by Miss Flatman of whom twenty-five have been firmly identified as Cheltenham women. Others are hard to identify because they have no initials and/or a common surname, but some may well have been from elsewhere as her sister, brother-in-law and niece from Surrey are in the list. These are those not already mentioned above:

---

10 Self-Denial weeks were annual events from 1908. Funds and/or goods were collected from women who were supposed to have sacrificed something for the cause.

Contributors to WSPU Funds

Name	Age	Address	Occupation	Contribution
Miss Mary Greeves(Greaves)	33	40 Montpellier Street	Private means	1s 1911, 2s 1912
Mrs Sophy Wishaw	71	Rock Holme, Leckhampton Hill	Private means, widow of merchant in Russia	5s 1911
Miss Mary Wishaw	35	ditto	Private means	£1 1911
Miss Ellen Sandy	37	Gloucester House	Children's nurse	2s 6d 1911
Miss Rolles (could be any one of three sisters)		Walsingham, Evesham Road	Private means	1s 1911
Nurse Violet Sanderson	33	Victoria Nurses' Home, St James' Square	Hospital trained nurse	4s 1911
Mrs Mabel Earwaker	48	Fern Lawn, Pittville Crescent	Wife of retired calico printer	2s 1911
Mrs Elizabeth King	41	Montrose, Wellington St.	Private means – widow of civil servant	1s 1911
Mrs Edith Mildmay	43	28 Park Place	Private means – widow of 'gentleman'	1s 1911
Mrs Julia Jones	63	1 Paragon Parade	Widow of Major General	£1 10s 1911
Mrs Mary Mushet	93	10 Sydenham Villas	Private means – widow	5s and £1 1911

The last lady in the list must have been one of the oldest WSPU supporters in the country! She was the widow of Robert Mushet who had made his fortune as the co-inventor of steel rails with Henry Bessemer. The couple came from the Forest of Dean but had lived in Cheltenham since he retired in the 1860s, having made his name and his money. They must have been happy there, although captains of industry were not common in Cheltenham society!

A woman who might have been from the lower ranks of society was Miss Thirza Ford, who held a meeting in her seven-roomed house in Montpellier Terrace in 1913. She was 65 and had 'private means', but in 1901 she was recorded as a needlewoman living in one room. Perhaps she had inherited money, for it is unlikely that she could make a considerable sum from even the best clientele within just ten years. An intriguing story must lurk beneath the facts. Did she become involved because she had experienced home-working for a pittance?

Fear and violence reach the town

Against a background of mounting WSPU violence, with arson attacks on empty buildings and government property and ingenious stunts like acid on golfing greens, the government was increasingly keen to suppress them. There had been police raids on their headquarters, and pursuit of prisoners released under the Cat and Mouse Act became more organised. The Home Office tried to seize material both to prosecute individuals and to reduce incitement to violence. As we have seen, Cheltenham was not a town which would have expected any outrages of this kind, and the women members seemed too involved in fundraising to consider more spectacular action. However, there were itinerant workers who were prepared to stage attacks anywhere in the country, as seen in the attack on Alstone Lawn described in Chapter 1.

The pages of *The Suffragette*, which replaced *Votes for Women* after the Pethick-Lawrences split from the Pankhursts in late 1912, recorded all incidents of arson or other sabotage, although one firm of printers was prosecuted for inciting violence and the WSPU kept having to seek alternative printers. Keeping the paper going was hard but was seen as a vital means of maintaining morale in the face of increasing government suppression. However, accounts of incidents were taken from the local newspapers and were subject to little editing. This meant that, where incidents were cited as the result of suffragette outrage, this was accepted without question: as there was some national hysteria about what the WSPU was doing, there were instances which were 'mis-reported' at local level.

Some Cheltenham incidents seem to have a strong WSPU connection. The first was at the Town Hall in August 1913. It was being redecorated and when one of the painters, Mr Charles Cossens, arrived, he found on the main steps a suspicious-looking object shaped like 'a tin lobster drum, about the size of the crown of a straw hat'. On it was painted in red 'Votes for Women'. It seems to have been 'ingeniously' fashioned with 'nine small cylinders each connecting with a fuse to the outside through the tube of a bicycle pump' (*Suffragette* 05/09/13). It contained black powder and there were spent matches lying nearby. Clearly, it had not worked and was perhaps harmless, as Mr Cossens was not greatly alarmed: he dismantled it, claiming to have been used to doing this in his army training. But the police took no chances and plunged it into water. The whole account by the *Chronicle* is light-hearted, talking of 'the nonchalance of the soldier-painter', and the workmen regarding it as 'fake'. The device may have been planted by someone wishing to blacken the suffragettes' name, but it was unlikely to have been a mere prank when such trouble was taken in its construction.

After the Alstone Lawn blaze in late December, there was a small spate of reported incidents, some of which may have been genuine, but it was the fear generated which was significant, as in any periods of terrorism. For example, *The Suffragette* reported in mid-January 1914 that: 'A large firm at Cheltenham, whose stock comprises many thousands of pounds' worth of timber, have made arrangements for a permanent night-watch of their premises, having in view the number of recent fires in the neighbourhood attributed to Suffragettes.'

This was certainly an exaggeration as, apart from Alstone Lawn, there seems only to have been one other, and that was quickly discounted as the result of suffragette activity. On 8 January, the relatively new buildings of the gymnasium and the adjoining geological and chemistry laboratories at St Paul's Training College went up in flames. It is a good example of how events could be exaggerated as the earliest accounts of the fire in the *Gloucestershire Echo* of 8 January, echoed in the *Chronicle* two days later, said: 'That it was not a Suffragette advertisement may be surmised from the fact that no literature of the type by which these ladies promulgate their theories was found.'

Fire at St Paul's College, Cheltenham, January 1913. There was speculation about whether the WSPU was responsible and their national newspaper used it as publicity. (Postcard in author's collection)

However, the *Gloucester Journal* account of 10 January suggested that it might have been 'incendiary suffragists' and *The Suffragette* of 16 January headlined this as 'Suffragettes Suspected'. The graphic accounts of the fire and the debris are accompanied by detail of how a number of causes were discounted: the boiler for heating, gas and electricity were all absolved, and the only clue was a key in a lock lying on the floor of the corridor leading to the geological laboratory. It appeared that someone had gained access.

Alongside the 8 January *Echo* account of the fire, there were details of another incident at Alstone Baths, which it is hinted might have been an attempted suffragette attack, although the writer admits that 'probably we are drifting into the habit of giving the militants credit for too much devilry nowadays'. The same light tone adopted by the local press over the Town Hall 'bomb' is used with a headline 'Did the pom. save Alstone Baths?' This is a reference to the little Pomeranian dog owned by the manager, Mr Pilkington, which barked in the early hours and may have scared off the intruder. The intruder was allegedly a woman because of the nature of the footmarks left on the garden and on a cushion inside, and a button from a lady's coat. Whoever it was, 'she' got through a window, climbed over the turnstile and made her way into the office, next door to the room where the dog was. The reporter decided that a common thief would have taken some equipment of value, even though there was no money in the office, and suggested that it might have been a suffragette intending to fire the building who did not leave any literature behind because she had to leave quickly!

The idea of an area besieged by attacks was sufficiently widespread for the *Echo* to run an article questioning how many local incidents were attributable to the suffragettes (10 January). There had been many apparent attacks in Bristol and South Wales at the time, on churches, cinemas, tea-rooms and a timber-yard. Was there a co-ordinated WSPU effort in the area?

The attitude to suffragettes and their alleged local outrages is so well expressed here, but in a balanced way, that it is worth including much of the article:

In spite of the Suffragettes having chosen beacon fires made with other people's private houses instead of the less picturesque methods of the bill-sticker to advertise their cause, in referring from time to time to the various ill deeds of which they are suspected, we are inclined to remember the lesson of the ironic essay by Goldsmith on mad dogs, and not to give credit to suspicions of further suffragette outrages every time a thrifty housewife saves the cost of a sweeper by firing her kitchen chimney. There are, however, various pieces of circumstantial evidence which seems to associate the ladies of the blazing firebrand with both the big fire at the Cheltenham Training College on Friday morning and some silly tricks played at the Gloucestershire Co-operative Society's chief Cheltenham shop in High-street.

During the dinner hour on Friday some person or persons unknown hacked off the coil of telephone wires running up the stairs of the Co-operative office … The wire was left twisted up on the stairs, and on a large notice-board faced with green baize was chalked the thrilling legend 'Votes for Women!'

The probability of somebody besides a militant feminist having chalked 'Votes for Women!' on any available area where it appears has become rather a large one, for creatures of lowly intelligence make up for wit by imitation … In the present instance, however, there have been other reasons to suppose that somebody wishes to start a blaze at the Co-operative shop, for quite recently, on several occasions, the gas has been found fully turned on without being lighted in some of the upstair rooms , and an explosion which might have blown the building from one side of the street to the other and killed a few score of people on the way has been narrowly averted. Consequently, the Co-operative people, without going into hysterics, or taking it altogether for granted that the Suffragette Philistines are upon them, are keeping their eyes open for their friends.

It has frequently been pointed out by the Suffragettes that they make a point in lighting their bonfires to select places which shall render them of no danger to human life. If that is so, the doings at the Co-operative Society's office must be set down to another class of pyromaniacs. In the case of the burning of the Training College, however, it is pointed out by those who favour the theory of a Suffragette origin of the fire, that just the time – the College being on vacation – and just the part of the building where life would be in least danger were chosen …

As far as we know there is no reason for supposing that St. Paul's has incurred the ire of the sisterhood, but that would not be taken as negative evidence, for in their other bonfires, like that at Alstone (Lawn), convenience for firing, rather than the thing fired, seems to have been the prevailing idea … Even the fact that no Suffragette literature was found does not throw off those who are on this clue. Had any been left in either of the buildings involved in the fire it would have been burnt; and it is possible, of course, as pointed out by one of the College staff to the writer, that the fire blazing up faster than was expected, personal safety rather than propaganda may have been the prevailing idea … as he or she bolted for the nearest way over the College wall.

The writer concludes by reporting that a large placard, bearing the words 'Votes for women; your turn next', was discovered attached to the rear entrance of the grammar school and was handed over to police. It was thought that the educational establishments of the town were taking 'precautions'.

So, the Cheltenham WSPU before the war did not end with a bang but a whimper! The last event recorded in the summer of 1914 was a drawing-room meeting at Dr Burn's house in Imperial Square, where there were brisk sales at the sweet stall for Self-Denial Week! By this time, Dr Burn was appearing at both WSS and CUWFA meetings and was more inclusive in her activities. Much of the early fervour had been lost but, as long as the Cheltenham branch continued, it bore witness to the militant movement nationally. And the fear of militancy in Cheltenham remained: it was reported that, at a Liberal meeting in the Town Hall, women were only permitted to sit in the balcony (*Looker-On* 20/6/14).

Cheltenham Suffragists Expand: Tewkesbury and Winchcombe Emerge

The WSS adapted to the presence of the WFL from 1908, partly as we have seen because some members straddled both groups. However, there were more challenges to come. The advent of the CUWFA in 1910, strengthened by the successful election of the pro-suffrage Conservative Agg-Gardner in 1911, meant that there were some defections. The greater number signing under the CUWFA heading in the 1912 book for Agg-Gardner indicates this. Additionally, the arrival of the WSPU in town in 1911, with the excitement of the by-election and the census avoidance campaign, took the spotlight off the suffragists. But throughout this the WSS kept going, sustained particularly by the continued presence and activism of Mrs Swiney and Miss Mills. So how did they maintain their momentum?

A gradual change?

An indication of an attempt to cultivate a wider membership is a 'daffodil concert' for 'working people' in April 1908 at Milsom-Street School, at the lower end of the High Street (*Echo* 14/04/08). The platform was decorated with daffodils which were given away at the end of the concert. Key figures in the society participated: Mrs Earengey (still part of the committee) spoke of the need for the vote, and she and Miss Boult performed a duologue on the subject. Mrs Mills gave two humorous readings and her daughter, in 'pseudo-Japanese dress', gave two costume songs – 'The poor little goldfish' and 'The little Jappy'. This somewhat patronising event speaks of good intentions but little real engagement with the more depressed section of the town.

The society continued trying to get support by holding public meetings with national figures when possible. So in 1909, they were able to advertise a meeting addressed by Sir John Cockburn, ex-premier of South Australia. The report of this meeting, submitted one presumes by Miss Mills, was very enthusiastic about its audience and the speaker, 'by far the best meeting ever held by the WSS locally' (*CC* 25/11/09). Sir John spoke with 'eloquence, vigour, humour and whole-hearted zeal' in comparing the situation in Australia with that of the mother country and Miss Mills commented that he was the best male speaker they had heard. She estimated that there were at least 500 people there, 'a large number of young women and men being present, Labour men[1] and thoughtful middle-class people', perhaps indicating they were attracting a wider audience than usual. There was also a whole front row of anti-suffragists, but they did not seem to have disrupted proceedings.

The nature of the audience does not seem to have increased the membership of the society. The AGM at the end of the year carried an appeal to party women to abandon their work for party and concentrate on the vote, and it was reported that only nine new members joined. A deputation of committee members to each parliamentary candidate for the general election proved that neither local candidate was willing to include women's suffrage in their election address, so reinforcing the need to abandon 'party'.[2]

A meeting with the WFL the next year on white slave traffic showed how the WSS was prepared to address social issues. General and Mrs Swiney held the first meeting by invitation in their own home, with sixty to seventy ladies present, to hear an address on 'Women's Suffrage and the Social Evil'. The second meeting in the Town Hall had an audience of 250–300 and was supported by a range of people, including the Rector of Cheltenham and Dr Grace Billings, who made the claim that the possession of the vote would help women to raise moral standards. Life was made more difficult for the WSS by the formal severing of membership ties with the WFL at the end of 1910, but co-operation was maintained.

The following year, 1911, was notable for its lack of public meetings, perhaps overshadowed by the WSPU activities in the census and by-election campaigns. However, somewhat under the radar of the local press, the WSS supported Agg-Gardner as the 'better Suffrage man' in the election and held both indoor and

---

1   Mr Butler, secretary of the ILP, gave the vote of thanks.

2   An impressive point was put to Lord Duncannon at his home in Douro Road at the first of these meetings. Dr Billings 'could deprive a man of his vote by signing a certificate of lunacy, but could not vote herself' (*Echo* 17/12/09).

outdoor gatherings to support him. This caused some Liberals to question the non-party attitude of the group, but they explained their position in friendly meetings and gained twelve new members (*CC* 23/05/11). As Conservatives had the CUWFA to represent them, it is likely that the WSS had a disproportionate number of Liberals now, in contrast to the position at the beginning of the century. That did not prevent Mr Agg-Gardner presiding at their 1911 AGM and thanking the society for supporting him in his by-election victory. The fact that he and Mrs Swiney disagreed over the action of the militants was passed over amicably.

One must beware of over-stressing party allegiance as, for many, it was irrelevant. However, a new factor arose in early 1912 when the national NUWSS made an electoral pact with the Labour Party. An Election Fighting Fund was set up to support Labour candidates in by-elections, in order to put more pressure on the Liberal government. We have seen that Cheltenham suffragists like Mrs Swiney had always had an interest in the concerns of the labouring classes, and this new national position seems to have had some effect on what they organised.

Before the pact was finalised, there had been a debate at the working-men's guild attended by Miss Mills. In February, the ILP held a meeting at which Keir Hardie was the speaker and Mrs Swiney and Miss Mills were on the platform. Keir Hardie, a close friend and lover of Sylvia Pankhurst, had long been an advocate of women's suffrage through his close association with the Pankhurst family and, unlike some of his Labour fellows, was prepared to campaign vigorously. Cheltenham Town Hall would not allow the meeting to be held on its premises on a Sunday afternoon, so it took place in the Drill Hall in Swindon Road. We do not know how much of Hardie's Cheltenham speech was devoted to women's suffrage as much attention was on the national miners' strike. However, in Gloucester, he spoke of how he would not vote for the government reform bill unless it included women's suffrage too.

His meeting had been preceded by a joint meeting with the WFL and the CUWFA, where Sir John Cockburn was again a speaker together with Mrs Philip Snowden, wife of the Labour MP, who was a passionate speaker for the cause. As the CUWFA also sponsored the meeting, it cannot be seen as party-political but there is an association with Labour which might not previously have been countenanced.

The other national development which reached out to lower-class supporters was the 'Friends' scheme, where women were encouraged to sign a card of support but did not have to make any commitment or pay membership. Cheltenham began this scheme in the summer of 1912 and later announced that forty had been signed up in the first year. One of the meetings at which the scheme was promoted was on women and elementary education where Miss Bathurst, who had been

Keir Hardie, Labour MP and visitor to Cheltenham to speak for the WSS in 1912. (Wikipedia, John Furley Lewis 1902)

an inspector for the Board of Education, spoke to teachers and others about the need for women to directly influence elementary education. The appeal was not to the many women engaged in private education, but to those working in schools for the less privileged. All this will have moved the WSS away from the social base it had in the early years of the century.

In early summer 1914, Cheltenham WSS entertained potentially its most controversial speaker, Rev. Hatty Baker. She was a pioneer woman preacher in the Congregational Church and had helped to found the Free Church League for Women's Suffrage in 1910. But her most recent step had been helping to inaugurate the first Women's Church in Wallasey, Cheshire, the Church of the New Ideal. This gave women the chance to run their own church and aimed to move God and Christ away from a masculine to a more feminine representation, notions which shocked many in 1914. Her speech to only a small audience in the supper room at the Town Hall did not emphasise the theological aspect too much. Instead, it concentrated on the social and moral aspects affecting women's lives, such as sweated labour, prostitution and drink, and unequal prison sentences. The solution to many problems was Christianity and the vote; Mrs Swiney endorsed this, saying 'it was because we had divorced religion from life and health that we found ourselves in such an unbalanced position' (*Echo* 18/05/14). Miss Mills also endorsed it, as she was there the next night when Rev. Baker preached at the Unitarian chapel on 'God, the Prior Mother of all'. Indeed, she sang for the occasion, as did Emmie Holloway, one of the sisters involved in the family photography business in Cambray who often performed at WSS social events. Surprisingly, no adverse comments about the visit can be found in the local press, except from an anti-suffrage supporter sometime later. Was Cheltenham prepared for such a radical stance?

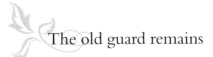

The old guard remains

The slight shift in emphasis of the WSS was accompanied by the continuing cultivation of the leisured classes. In 1909, it was suggested that they should hold 'At Homes' where a lady would offer to host a meeting, usually in her own home. The difference between these and drawing-room meetings was negligible and many societies, constitutional and militant, had used them for some years.

In Cheltenham, the first was held at the home of Mrs and Miss Mills. Obviously, these meetings would be held in the homes of the better-off and the first few show this. The Misses Ransford and Miss Truby hosted one at their home in Halland Road, Leckhampton. All three women were of 'private means' but were not of the

Cheltenham WSS Garden Party in Mrs Swiney's garden, Sandford Lawn, Bath Road. Miss Theodora Mills, secretary, Mrs Swiney, president, and Rev. J. Smith, Unitarian minister. In the background is the banner held by the Cheltenham Trust. (*Cheltenham Chronicle and Gloucestershire Graphic*, 23 July 1910)

colonial/military class and their house was not grand. Both Misses Ransford had been hospital matrons in 1901 but were the daughters of a wealthy grocer. They therefore had money and experience of working in positions of responsibility, but were not deemed worthy of the vote. The room was filled with many women, 'almost all of whom were interested outsiders', and 'a dainty tea' was served. Mrs Swiney's address was perhaps targeting a specific audience as she spoke of the importance of the vote for working women but, as it was an afternoon meeting, it is unlikely that any of the women were workers.

Others were held at the home of long-term committee member Mrs Seaforth Mackenzie, who was the wife of a wealthy woollen merchant and lived in Montpellier Grove, and at the home of Mrs Isabel and Miss Alfreda Browett, of Tivoli Road. They were a widowed mother and daughter whose husband/father had been a Birmingham silversmith and electro-plate manufacturer. Therefore, all of these hostesses, including the Mills, were from trade or commercial backgrounds, so perhaps they do after all represent a slight shift in class basis.

Alongside these meetings to attract interest and new members in a comfortable domestic atmosphere were the customary garden parties. The venues for these annual events had to be the gardens of even larger houses and one imagines the social buzz which would have surrounded them. Mrs Arscot Lowenfeld, a lady much involved in the social and charitable life of the town, welcomed the event in the grounds of her twenty-roomed house in The Park (Oakfield) in 1905. Mrs Swiney took on the responsibility in 1909 and 1910, and there is a picture from 1910 showing her and a rather demure Miss Mills listening to the fiery Unitarian Rev. Smith in front of one of the ever-present banners!

In 1911, the venue was the fourteen-roomed Mellington, London Road, Charlton Kings, where Mrs Aimee Gibbons lived with her husband, a retired lieutenant colonel from the Indian Medical Service. In 1914, a thunderstorm intervened and the intended party at Miss Jessie Bourne's 'beautiful house', Ashmead Lodge on Leckhampton Hill, had to be moved inside. Even in a house of thirteen rooms, this may have been a squash![3] It was on this occasion that Lady Isabel Margesson, a frequent speaker at Cheltenham meetings, gave a 'deeply moving address' (CC 26/06/14). It is not known what was so 'moving' but she had often

---

3 Jessie Bourne was listed as a teacher in the 1901 census, but her stepfather was a wealthy retired bedstead maker! She was therefore another woman who had tasted the world of work and independence before, with her mother and sister, inheriting money in her mid-forties. Her mother and sister were also supporters.

spoken passionately about the needs of poor mothers and children. She had been the principal speaker at the 1909 party when she defended militants; she told of how her daughter Catherine had been arrested at a meeting when the police were 'ordered to play football with them'. She had witnessed the rough treatment and, though not a suffragette, she 'honoured and loved those noble women who were willing to suffer the deepest humiliation' (*Examiner* 22/07/09).

It is interesting that, in spite of having sympathy with the militants, she was still being invited to speak at suffragist meetings – could this have been because of her social position? This is possible, as there was some friction within the Cheltenham WSS which surfaced earlier in 1914. A members-only meeting was called at which Miss Gardiner proposed a motion condemning militancy which was seconded by Miss Bourne, in whose house Lady Margesson was to speak.[4] Mrs Swiney and others opposed the motion, but it was carried. A month later, this was taken further when Miss Helena Heath, a long-term committee member (a wealthy lady of Wellesley Court, Clarence Square, whose father had been a clergyman), proposed that anyone who supported militancy should be excluded from membership. The seconder was Mrs Elsie Jones, whose absentee husband, Arthur, was the editor of the daily English-language paper in India, *The Statesman*. This did not bind her to the views of Mrs Swiney, also with strong Indian connections: Mrs Swiney again opposed the motion and her views won the day (*CC* 24/04/14). While expressions of regret about militant excesses had always been allowed at WSS meetings, Mrs Swiney had on occasion been prepared to back WSPU action and condemn police action. She was not prepared to concede her right, or the right of others, to do this, nor did she seem afraid of a division of opinion. One wonders whether the ladies who had opposed her were at the Garden Party to hear Lady Margesson. Had the war not intervened, the local WSS cracks might have grown wider.

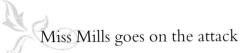

Miss Mills goes on the attack

As had happened in previous years, the WSS in 1912 embarked on campaigning visits to outlying villages. Miss Mills mentioned Deerhurst, Churchdown, Badgeworth, Hatherley, Reddings (sic) and Hilcot in her report, but with no details of success

---

4 Probably Miss Gardiner was the retired schoolmistress who had in 1911 supported the WSPU by chairing a meeting. The escalation of militancy did alienate some women.

or otherwise. In September, Cheltenham was visited by the NUWSS van! The idea of sending a caravan touring round different parts of the country, usually to rural or seaside areas, for propaganda purposes had been adopted by both the WFL and the NUWSS in 1908. The visit of 1912 came at the end of a tour which was moving from the Welsh borders through Kidderminster and Pershore to the final engagement before making its way home. It had not been a happy tour in its latter stages, as the tent with the caravan was flooded in the Welsh borderland.

However, Miss Mills reported to the *Looker-On* (21/09/12) that the visit had been successful: 'a capital meeting was held at Prestbury … when as a result of merely an hour's canvass an excellent audience came together in the main street … The ground had been prepared all thro(sic) this countryside by the previous distribution of Suffrage leaflets at 24 villages.' She also reported an orderly meeting of 130 adults at the Clarence Street Lamp to hear Miss Gill, the principal speaker. Imagine her horror on reading the Van report in *The Common Cause*, which claimed that 'This week's meetings were the least satisfactory we had on the whole tour'! Maybe the view was coloured by the fact that the weather suddenly became very cold and they abandoned the horse and van in a field outside the town and retreated to Gardiner's Hotel (sic)! (This was Gardner's Hotel, Clarence Parade.)

A WSS touring caravan and tent – this is what the one which visited Cheltenham in 1912 would have looked like. (Women's Library postcard, London School of Economics)

Miss Mills was not prepared to let this criticism in the national suffrage press stand. She swung into action immediately and a letter defending Cheltenham appeared the next week. She claimed that the meeting at the lamp was even better than reported, with a crowd as large as that at the by-election. She blamed the failure of three meetings on the speaker's illness and 'unusual harvest conditions and unlooked-for village outings'. She also seemed to blame Miss Gill, the chief van-speaker, for the near-fiasco at Prestbury as she had given the handbills to be distributed to the Gordon Boys' Home, 'the result of all which was that no bills whatever were given out'.[5]

The truth of some of this was affirmed by Vera Collum, the driver of the van, in the same issue. However, she made a sideways swipe at the fact that they had not met any of the Cheltenham members apart from Miss Mills and Mrs Swiney. Had more been able to help, the visit might have been more successful. Not to be outdone, Miss Mills sent another letter the next week disputing the figure of three or four adults at the Prestbury meeting, when she had counted twenty-five before she left. Had there only been that number, the meeting would not have been held as, at Churchdown, a meeting of ten was cancelled. This is a determined Miss Mills, concerned that the Cheltenham branch should not be seen in a bad light.

Disgraceful scenes in Cheltenham

The event which caused the most aggression and damaged the reputation of the town occurred in July 1913, when the NUWSS Pilgrimage arrived. The Pilgrimage set off to converge on four main routes to London to raise awareness of and support for the constitutional suffragists. Although it had been planned beforehand, it happened in the wake of the huge publicity surrounding the death of the WSPU's Emily Davison at the Epsom Derby, with her subsequent funeral procession bringing much of London to a stop. Sympathy was gained for the

---

5   She is referring to the Gordon Boys' Brigade which was effectively a home for disadvantaged boys in Liverpool Place, just off the High Street where John Lewis is now building a store. Boys were given accommodation and food while learning how to earn money by running errands and doing jobs for local residents, but Miss Mills did not think very highly of them! The 1912 Annual Report spoke of the excellent discipline and 'energy and zeal' of the boys, many of whom moved into apprenticeships on leaving.

The routes taken by the NUWSS Pilgrimage in the summer of 1913. While the names of the places are indistinct, it is possible to see how Cheltenham and Cirencester linked into the main routes. (*The Common Cause*, 27 June 1913)

cause, but also much anger at WSPU tactics of increasing militancy. Nothing had happened in Cheltenham to raise alarm, so it is surprising that the arrival of the peaceful Pilgrimage by the non-militant suffragists caused such uproar.

It was planned as a kind of 'cascade' journey where groups of local supporters would join the march for a short time as it passed through their area: it was not expected that all women would go the whole way, although it was hoped that its arrival in London would be accompanied by the arrival of many thousands of supporters. The women travelled in a variety of ways, some walked, some cycled and some used brakes, carts or motor cars. It was suggested that they wore a 'uniform' of grey, white, black or navy coats or skirts and dresses, with a white shirt. The publicity they gained was invaluable but, at some places, including Cheltenham, Cirencester and Swindon, onlookers failed to distinguish them from the militants or there was an orchestrated demonstration by the 'Antis'.

Women walking on the NUWSS Pilgrimage. (*The Common Cause*, 27 June 1913)

On 15 July, two charabancs of pilgrims arrived from Gloucester, with some following on foot. The procession lined up in Lansdown Road with a wagonette carrying the local leaders, Mrs Swiney, Miss Mills and Rev. J.H. Smith, the Unitarian minister, all WSS, and Dr Alice Burn of the WSPU who, by this time, was also associating herself with the CUWFA and WSS. 'The pilgrims wore a green badge on the arm, with the name of the town from which they marched in red letters; some also wore sashes in the colours for hats' (*Journal* 19/07/13). It had the potential to be a happy colourful event.

The fullest and most vivid account in the *Echo* of 16 July is sympathetic to those involved and horrified by the reaction they received. A crowd of several hundreds, mainly 'youths and hobbledehoys', was waiting for them at the Clarence Street Lamp and violence erupted as soon as they arrived. They were rushed at and a banner was seized and broken. Mrs Swiney and Rev. Smith were both denied a hearing by shouting, 'leather-banging' and the jangling of a hand-bell. Only the efforts of the police prevented the wagonette being overturned at one point and then eggs were thrown, hitting both Mrs Swiney and Rev. Smith. Eventually, after the horse was nearly pushed off its legs, the coachman became alarmed and more missiles were thrown, the police persuaded the speakers to give up. They drove towards the High Street, followed by a 'howling mob' as far as Wellington Street, while those on foot were chased until they found shelter in the police station. Two women from Gloucester were pulled off their bicycles after sheltering in Mr Wright's cigar shop at the corner of County Court Road, and were pinned against the railings outside the telephone exchange until rescued by seven policemen. Miss Mills said that some of the mob followed the wagonette as far as Mrs Swiney's house in Bath Road, although the police formed a cordon to try to keep the crowd at bay. Most of the pilgrims from outside the town returned to Gloucester in charabancs. She herself did not try to speak and she does not record any offence to herself, although her later experiences in the Pilgrimage were less comfortable (see Cirencester chapter). In a letter of 1938, she described how her frail mother, weighing only 6½ stone, was in the wagonette when things were being thrown and she had to be lifted down by a policeman (*Echo* 18/07/38). Her obsession with the banners is again evident as she said that one of the banners was stolen, but luckily 'not the green cloth and velvet' one used at public meetings (*Echo* 13/02/18).

Both the *Echo* reporters who described the scenes condemned the 'gangs of hooligans and loafers' together with some men and women who should have known better, and one commended the actions of 'respectable artisans' who tried to protect the women. One of them merely hinted that the 'Antis' were behind the disturbances but this is not substantiated, and both insisted that some people were unable or unwilling to distinguish between suffragists and suffragettes. The editorial pursued this further and yet regretted that 'a portion of blame must be borne by the law-abiding suffragists' shrieking sisters who have brought their cause into disrepute and who, though frequently well educated women, have given the rougher element so bad an example.'

'Outreach' work – Tewkesbury and Winchcombe

Although Tewkesbury, like Cheltenham, Cirencester and Stroud, had a history of some activity in the 1870s and 1880s, there was no established society and much of the impetus seems to have come from Mrs Harriet McIlquham, whose home in Staverton meant that she looked towards both Cheltenham and Tewkesbury. In the early twentieth century, there was little sign of home-grown activity.

Some debates on the topic were organised by men's societies and outsiders attempted to whip up some interest. The most noteworthy was the arrival of a group of four NUWSS ladies from Oxford to hold a meeting at the Cross in June 1909, only to be barred by a policeman! The leader, Miss Rachel Costelloe,[6] had

---

6   Better known as Ray Strachey after her marriage to the brother of Lytton Strachey in 1911. Author of *The Cause*, a history of the women's movement.

gone into the police station to ask permission to hold the meeting and speak from their motor car: Inspector Keyes refused. He was obviously keen to prevent this at all costs as, when he went outside to see where they were parked, he noticed that the rear number plate was obscured by a mackintosh with the words 'National Union Women's Suffrage Society'. She was therefore prosecuted for the offence and misleadingly labelled a 'suffragette' in the proceedings (*Echo* 02/07/09). Clearly, there had been no prior arrangement for the meeting and no local involvement.

From 1911, initiatives were taken by Cheltenham-based individuals and the constitutional societies to support and incentivise Tewkesbury activity. The regional organiser of the NUWSS, Kate Robertson, also made it one of her targets. One of the main concerns was that the MP Michael Hicks-Beach was not in favour of women's suffrage and had spoken against it in 1909. As the Conservative Cheltenham MP Agg-Gardner was a champion of the cause, the Cheltenham branch of the CUWFA felt impelled to do some 'outreach' work. In May 1911, Flora Kelley, the secretary, and Miss Anne Welch of Arle Court went to the House of Commons to see Hicks-Beach and ask for his support for the Conciliation Bill. All he would promise was to be guided by the course of the debate. As far as we know, no Tewkesbury residents were involved in the deputation.

The lack of interest is evident in Kate Robertson's frustration in trying to form a WSS branch. She wrote:

> Very little is known about Suffrage there, and most of the people on whom I called did not even know that there was a National Union. In most cases it was quite obvious that any information give[n] on the subject was received with a mental reservation …There are some real sympathiser[s] in Tewkesbury, and from these we met with a great deal of kindness. Miss Haffner, headmistress of the Trinity Infant School, very kindly took the classes of each of the teachers in turn in order that we might have a few minutes' talk with them.
>
> (*CC* 21/09/11)

Miss Thirza Haffner, a lady in her forties living with her widowed mother in Ashchurch Road, went out of her way to be supportive when this might have been frowned upon by her employers. But Miss Robertson was treading water in the town: in October, a meeting at the Watson Memorial Hall had a very poor audience and she commented 'Tewkesbury wants prodding' (*CC* 26/10/11).

However, all was not lost in terms of the parliamentary constituency, because Winchcombe had an enthusiastic band of supporters. This enabled a branch to be formed, called the Tewkesbury Division branch but used interchangeably with

'Winchcombe' in the suffrage press reports. The only reference to activity before 1911 is a rather 'twee' account (*CC* 17/10/09), obviously written by Miss Mills. In a light-hearted way, she describes how all along the main street:

> heads were being thrust out of doors and people appeared talking to each other and gazing after the form of two women who moved from house to house, knocking, leaving mysterious leaflets and making a certain announcement … At four o'clock a little knot of men and women and a large crowd of perfectly well behaved children gathered in the central space known variously as the Queen's Square and the Wide Walk. Here a banner appeared, and while one Suffragist hovered about (successfully) to dispose of penny pamphlets, the other mounted on a backless chair with one wobbly leg and talked for an hour … Altogether over thirty adults must have heard some part of the message. All were quiet and attentive. A plain-clothes policeman cycled up towards the end, evidently sent hastily from distant headquarters, and … gently informed the speaker that her rostrum was an 'obstruction' on the pavement, and must be stood two yards away in the road.

The origin of the support for a branch to be formed seemed to have been the taking of five people's names as a result of a visit by the Miss Mills and two national speakers during the Cheltenham by-election campaign earlier in the year. The five names are not given but may include the first president, Miss Mabel Malleson of Dixton Manor, Alderton. She was in her fifties, Cambridge-educated and briefly a history teacher, the daughter of Elizabeth Malleson, a veteran of women's causes. Mrs Malleson had been a founder-member of the Ladies' London Emancipation Society and founded the Working Women's College but her daughter Hope was, to her mother's disappointment, a member of the WSPU. So Mabel Malleson was steeped in the women's movement.[7]

Also likely to have been in the initial five were the first joint secretaries of the branch, Miss Amie and Miss Rosie Livens of Timber House. They were the young daughters of the landscape and floral still-life painter Henry Livens. Both were described as Art Students in the 1911 census and it is known that Amie went on to be known as the 'painting nun' when she joined a convent in Finchley! As

---

7   Interestingly, she was also a friend of the actress Ellen Terry, who was a member of the Actresses' Franchise League (AFL).

time went on, it was Miss Rosie who seemed to have taken the chair at meetings and was more prominent, although only 19 when she was first appointed. She took to the letters page of the *Examiner* (09/01/13) when she felt that a debate at Winchcombe had been unfairly reported. This had taken place at the end of 1912 and Miss Malleson had spoken, as she had at the Cheltenham AGM. Her sister Amie also picked up her pen to the *Chronicle* to demonstrate the degree of local Liberal support in the town, with both the women's and men's sections carrying women's suffrage resolutions overwhelmingly (04/01/13).

The close association between Cheltenham and Winchcombe is further shown by the way in which Winchcombe supporters made their way to Cheltenham to sign the book of thanks to Agg-Gardner in 1912. Apart from Miss Malleson, another three have been identified. Mr Edward Adlard signed under the CUWFA section. He was in charge of the paper manufacturing company at Postlip Mills. His business partner, Francis Bird, was also involved in the movement – he gave the vote of thanks at a meeting in 1914. Miss (Nellie) Adelaide Mason made the journey to Cheltenham, apparently on her own; she was in her early twenties and lived in North Street, assisting in her grandmother's grocery business. She signed as a 'Sympathiser' which suggests that she perhaps could not afford membership of one of the societies.

Three other ladies associated with the constituency signed: Mrs Grace Healing, the wife of a wealthy flour miller of Avonside, Tewkesbury, signed as a sympathiser. Mrs Louisa Grice-Hutchinson signed as a WSS member and was often on platforms in the area in the years immediately before the war. She lived in style with seven servants at The Boynes, Upton-on-Severn, and was the widow of a retired army officer and Conservative MP. Her contacts with the army/political elite in Cheltenham can be imagined. Mrs Sarah Anne Mercier, who lived in similar style in Kemerton, signed as a CUWFA member. She was the widow of the rector and, after some controversy, had bought the right to appoint his successor to maintain the high-church tradition in the village – she appointed her son!

Further representation to Hicks-Beach was supported by Cheltenham CUWFA. For example, led again by Miss Kelley, the Cheltenham secretary, there was a CUWFA/NUWSS deputation to him while he was resident at Sudeley Castle in October 1912 (*Examiner* 31/10/12). Mrs Mercier was part of it, as was another CUWFA Cheltenham man, Richard Bagnall-Oakeley, who travelled over Cleeve Hill from Edgbaston House, Prestbury. The deputation crossed party lines and had the support of the local Liberal Association, as Amie Livens had suggested in her letter to the *Chronicle*. Named Liberals were Dr Earengey (now president of Winchcombe WSS, a local Liberal councillor, still living and working in Cheltenham) and Miss

Sexty of Isbourne House, Castle Street, a member of the Liberal Association and WSS committee member.[8] They were joined by another Winchcombe man, Mr Hubert Woodward of North Street, who was the Poor Law relieving officer, a more modest background. This breadth of opinion had little effect on Hicks-Beach: he used the 'thin edge of the wedge' argument that even a small step towards women's suffrage would lead to all kinds of unacceptable proposals.

The following year, 1913, seems quieter, although a lack of reports does not mean that there was a lack of activity on the ground. There was perhaps disagreement about tactics as, at the AGM at the end of the year, both the Misses Livens and Miss Sexty resigned from the committee. In discussion of the future work of the branch, it was felt that, because of 'considerable apathy' in the country districts 'and that a certain section of local public opinion had not yet completely recovered from the irritation aroused by the Militants' campaign of arson, it was decided to postpone for some months any attempt to get up a large public meeting, and for the moment, to concentrate upon quiet propaganda work' (*CC* 16/01/14). This meant a special effort in the villages, with leafletting explaining that they were not militants, the enrolling of 'Friends' and the holding of drawing-room and garden meetings. The concern not to upset the locality was relatively successful, as the membership rose from twenty-six to thirty-six in the next six months. The town had been divided into districts with one person taking charge of each, and one on a bicycle taking on the nearby villages! However, there are suggestions that the branch had nearly been dissolved and only the encouragement of Dr Earengey had kept them going.

It still needed support from Cheltenham, which it had in the person of Dr Earengey and visits from Miss Kelley. She and Dr Burn were willing to perform their duologue *A Chat with Mrs Chicky* whenever they could, and Winchcombe 'working men and women' appreciated it. The two women had become expert at using it as a means of propaganda. We know that they also performed at Tewkesbury, Cirencester, and were invited to the Cheltenham Food Reform Association so perfected it for performing anywhere!

A Chat with Mrs Chicky by Evelyn Glover was first performed in London in early 1912, and aimed to poke fun at the 'Antis' and to show that the vote was as relevant to working-class women as to the middle and upper classes. It had propaganda and entertainment value. The selection of audiences by Miss Kelley and Dr Burn

---

8   Miss Emily and Miss Kate Sexty were joint heads of household, in their fifties, and living on the money made by their deceased father, a tanner, currier and leather merchant.

is therefore interesting. Mrs Chicky is a charwoman, poor and uneducated, and Mrs Holbrook is an anti-suffrage canvasser collecting signatures across the classes to send to a newspaper. She assumes that she can browbeat Mrs Chicky into signing, but Mrs Chicky puts up a spirited defence and presents arguments which make Mrs Holbrook look foolish. Her concluding speech is a triumph. Talking about the first woman speaker she heard, she says:

> She didn't waste no time tellin' women 'oo'd sent their lads off to fight with their own 'earts breakin' for all their lips were smilin', as women 'ad't no feelins for their country an' didn't understand nothin' about war! She didn't waste no time tellin' sweated women drove on the streets – women 'oo's 'usbands give 'em a drib 'ere an' a drab there when they're sober, an' the childring goin' 'alf-naked – women 'oo's 'usbands take up with another woman, an' 'I'm afraid the lo can't 'elp you my good woman' says 'Is Wushup, in nine cases outer ten – women 'oo get drove to despair with facin' their trouble alone while the man 'oo's brought 'em to it gets off scot-free – women 'oo'll take on their 'usband's job when 'e's ill, to keep the 'ome goin', an' get eight or ten shillins docked off for the same amount of work cos they aint men … Oh, I'm not sayin' this 'ere vote's goin' to set everythin' right, but I do say as anythin' that's done without it'll be just patchin' an' nothin' more! It's goin' to make women COUNT!

Dr Burn would be more acquainted with working-class speech than Miss Kelley, who had led a very sheltered life, so she was Mrs Chicky – but we do not know how talented they were as actresses. At the Winchcombe meeting, Dr Burn also talked about sex equality in her native New Zealand and this all 'made a deep impression on a number of working-class girls, who had hitherto taken no interest in the movement' (*CC* 24/07/14).

Tewkesbury itself, however, had never collected sufficient support to establish a separate WSS branch. Apart from the efforts in 1911 made by Miss Robertson, very little emerges about activity in the town. Cheltenham CUWFA again held a meeting at the Watson Hall in March 1912, when the *Echo* of 7 March headed the report 'NO SYMPATHY WITH MILITANTS'. However, there was no representation from the town on the platform or in the vote of thanks. Similarly, at a joint CUWFA/WSS meeting at The Abbey Schoolroom in January 1914, Dr Alice Burn spoke and she and Miss Kelley performed their usual duologue. The hostesses were Mrs Grice-Hutchinson (see above) and Lady Maud Parry, wife of composer Hubert Parry, and living at Highnam Court. Oddly in a meeting largely dominated by the CUWFA, Lady Parry chose to commend the Labour Party for its attitude to women's suffrage. An audience of about 100 was reported and several members joined both societies, but it was stated that most of the success was due to Miss Kelley (*CC* 16/01/14 and *Journal* 17/01/14).

While the 'outreach' work may have been of limited success in Tewkesbury, it indicates the strength of the Cheltenham groups which could afford the woman-power to do this. It would not have been entirely unselfish: they wanted a friendlier neighbouring MP to support the cause in Parliament.

10

CIRENCESTER: AN UPHILL STRUGGLE

Mrs Pankhurst in Cirencester

While Cirencester had some women's suffrage impetus of its own, it also owed much to events in Cheltenham. When a national WSPU organiser was sent from headquarters to galvanise the movement, it was expected that she would campaign in the surrounding area. So, when Ada Flatman thought she had firmly established a branch in Cheltenham, she moved to Cirencester in June 1911, taking up residence at 12 Ashcroft Villas, a lodging house run by Miss Ella Jaques. She issued a plea for help with her campaign, urging volunteers to come and spend a holiday 'in this pretty place' (*VFW* 16/06/11). There was not a single member in Cirencester and she felt there was much work to be done to rouse the people's interest. But she already knew that the central point of the campaign would be the visit by Mrs Pankhurst on 6 July.

In support of this, she held preliminary drawing-room meetings, a usual method of recruiting the wealthier women. Immediately coming to the fore in the town were two ladies: Mrs Evelyn Dives of 28 Cecily Hill, whose husband Frederick Thomas was a 'director', possibly of his wife's family business, had a meeting at which a number of new subscribers were gained for *Votes for Women*, the WSPU weekly newspaper. She also canvassed for support for the Pankhurst meeting. Mrs Maud Melville of Stratton Firs,[1] the young wife of George Melville, a lawyer and

---

1 Later of Stratton House, now Stratton House Hotel. Mrs Melville was obviously a woman of spirit. A newspaper account in 1918 tells of how she rode her bicycle in Cirencester without lights at 10.45 p.m. and refused to appear at court to answer the charges, a court headed by one of the local anti-suffrage campaigners, Mr William Cole (*Echo* 16/07/18).

Mrs Evelyn Dives of Cecily Hill, Cirencester, one of the WSPU sympathisers, welcoming Mrs Pankhurst to the town. (Suffragette Fellowship Archive © Museum of London)

landowner, invited her friends to discuss the issues and also lent her motor car to reach rural residents. Whether these two ladies had any previous allegiance to the movement is unknown, but they were clearly not afraid to put themselves into the public arena.

The local newspaper, the *Wiltshire and Gloucestershire Standard*, warned the local residents of what was to come, in a somewhat ambiguous tone. In an article of 17 June, which Ada Flatman had kept in her scrapbook of the campaign, it stated: 'Ciceter must prepare itself for being awakened. So far Miss Flatman has confined herself to personal calls, interviews, and explaining to drawing room meetings and garden parties arranged by sympathisers or those open to conviction the reasons for the movement and the arguments on which it is based.' It then spoke of the 'redoubtable' Mrs Pankhurst's imminent arrival and appeared to praise the 'vigour of the militant suffragists that they should pursue their agitation at this time of year, in this weather, and regardless of the Coronation (of George V) and other preoccupations'. However, the veiled warning appears at the end when it states that 'we mention this merely to show what women can and will do when they are in earnest, and in order that Ciceter may not be taken too violently by surprise when it finds itself the field of full Suffragette activity.' The key word here may be 'violently'. While not openly hostile to the suffragettes, it may have been that the anti-suffrage stance of the dominant local aristocracy, the Bathursts, was something of which the local press had to be wary.

Mrs Pankhurst at Cirencester. The photograph was taken very close to Mrs Dives' house at the top of Cecily Hill. (Postcard in author's collection, photographer W. Dennis Moss)

An open-air meeting in the Market Place was held three days before Mrs Pankhurst's meeting, advertised by pavement writing, and the *Standard* reported that there was quite a large crowd. Ada Flatman addressed the meeting and 'satisfactorily answered several questions'. Tickets for 6 July were available from Messrs Baily and Woods (a private subscription library and publishers) in the Market Place, and it is fortunate that Miss Flatman kept samples of these and a flyer in her scrapbook.

What is also a coup for the area is that some charming photographs of Mrs Pankhurst were taken in Cirencester by W. Dennis Moss, probably all issued as postcards. As he was a self-employed photographic artist who lived at 24 Cecily Hill, it is likely that his proximity to Mrs Dives allowed these artistically posed pictures to be taken nearby. (They may have been taken on different occasions in the same visit, as she has a longer cape in my postcard than in others.)

Another stroke of luck for the researcher is that, in Ada Flatman's collection, she has named some of the people, so we are able to identify Mrs Dives. The car was a big Wolseley that Mrs Pankhurst was given by Miss Mary Hodge, an American copper-mining heiress who had come to live in London and supported the militant movement.[2] The car was used during the spring and summer of 1911 for Mrs Pankhurst to tour the country, and her chauffeur, Aileen Preston, has recalled in some detail her experiences of this.[3] Having undergone a mechanics and

2 For example, she gave Ethel Smyth, the suffragette and composer, £100 a year for life (J. Purvis: *Emmeline Pankhurst*, p.157).

The Unitarian minister Rev. Austin's Golden Wedding. He and his wife had been long-term supporters of women's suffrage in Cirencester. (*Gloucester Journal*, 31 May 1913)

driving course, she was the first woman to pass the RAC motoring certificate:[4] she then advertised in the *Morning Post* for a job and the WSPU responded. She describes how large the car was after what she was used to, 'a pantechnicon', and how she often had to transport five women, their baggage and literature in the dry, hot summer. At the point when the photograph was taken, she was just 22 years of age but was regarded as more reliable than the previous driver, Vera Holme, whom Mrs Pankhurst thought 'giddy' (M. Pugh: *The Pankhursts*, p. 153). Knowledge of the mechanics of a car was necessary for driving in more remote areas – punctures and over-heating were common – and Aileen Preston had that knowledge. She loved the job and thought the £1 a week wage was real wealth.

The preparation and publicity for the meeting was doubtless very efficient and enthusiastic, but how would the citizenry of a town as yet untouched by the movement react? The *Cheltenham Chronicle and Gloucestershire Graphic* of 8 July had obviously asked the same question. Their reporter answered that 'Happily, Cirencester stood well to her past traditions of fair play to all, and the meeting was of a successful and enthusiastic character, while the attendance was much larger and more representative than was generally expected.'

---

3   BBC *Woman's Hour* archives have a recording of 1962, for example.
4   This is according to her 1962 account. Other authorities have suggested that it was an AA certificate.

The reporter for the *Standard* gives some idea of local notables in the audience. Professor J.R. and Mrs Ainsworth-Davis head the list and, as he was Principal of the Agricultural College at the time, this was a presence which would not be lost on the town's society. Mrs Adamthwaite lived in great comfort at Siddington Lodge (her husband was living on 'private means' according to the 1911 census). She had links with the Ainsworth-Davises.[5] Also part of that 'set' was Mr R.K. Swanwick, who lived at College Farm and was a farmer and colliery director. The one person listed whose long-term support for the cause can be established was the Rev. Henry Austin, who was the Unitarian minister of the church in Gosditch Street, living at Cleeve Hill, Stratton, in 1911. Rev. Austin had been chair of a women's suffrage society in Cirencester as far back as the early 1870s. As can be seen in Cheltenham with Rev. Smith, Unitarianism and the women's suffrage movement were often companions. The reporter's 'etc.' at the end of the list is frustrating, as presumably there were more of 'the great and the good' of local society who could have been named!

The chairman was Rev. Geoffrey Ramsey, the Rector of Writhlington in Somerset. Why a more local chairman was not chosen is not known. On the platform, apart from Miss Flatman, were Mrs Dives from Cecily Hill (see above) and Mrs Robert Hobbs, the wife of a Kelmscot farmer, who mentioned in a question at the end that she was a member of another women's suffrage society. Rev. G.S.S. Vidal, who was the Rector of Barnsley (Glos.), was on the platform. His wife was one of those named in the audience and she seems to have been an Irish lady of ingenuity, as the 1911 census shows that she was a chocolate maker at home in the rectory! Some of the 'great and the good' from Cirencester and its hinterland had therefore not flinched at making their interest public.

Rev. Ramsey gave a rousing introduction to Mrs Pankhurst, calling her 'the prophetess and the priestess of the great movement, and the greatest woman of the nation'. But he also unequivocally stated that there would be no national progress without the 'intelligent and the ethical contribution of womanhood'. As a Church of England clergyman, it was his duty to speak out plainly on 'any movement which would tend to make the world better and happier than it was at present'. Mrs Pankhurst replied that she was 'in a town that somehow or other had been out of the current of this very great movement', a statement that was later to be corroborated with feeling by the leader of the Cirencester suffragists, Grace Hadow. She made

---

5   Her son Hugh was best man at the wedding of their daughter two years later.

Advertisement by the enterprising Mrs Constance Vidal, wife of the Vicar of Barnsley, Glos. They both attended Mrs Pankhurst's meeting in Cirencester and seem to have been supportive. (*Kelly's Directory*, Cirencester, 1913)

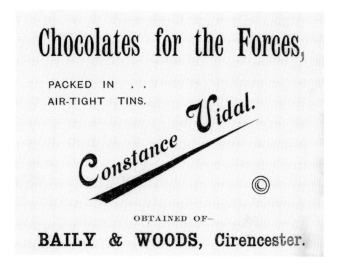

Chocolates for the Forces,

PACKED IN . .
AIR-TIGHT TINS. *Constance Vidal.*

©

OBTAINED OF—

BAILY & WOODS, Cirencester.

it clear that none of the women's societies was seeking the vote for all women but equality with the men's voting qualifications, particularly as many women paid taxes but had no say in how those taxes were spent. She emphasised that women did not want to become like men but wanted their different perspective and experiences to contribute to the nation. 'Women realised that laws were constantly being made that affected them and their interests; they realised that there was a great deal of wrong that ought to be put right, and that a great many mistakes were made, not from bad feeling but from a lack of knowledge.'

After the warm applause for Mrs Pankhurst's speech, Ada Flatman outlined the future programme locally and announced that there would be a 'memorial' to be signed by women municipal voters. She then adopted a more provocative tone by saying that she understood that they had an MP (Hon. Benjamin Bathurst, Conservative) who did not approve of women's suffrage. 'Well, the women municipal voters could tell him that next year they would be his constituents, as they most probably would be, and he would no doubt think twice before he said that he was not in favour of Women's suffrage.' This kind of challenge was not well received by the Bathurst coterie as will be seen.

There were also some challenging questions to Mrs Pankhurst herself, two of which were amusing on the surface but could have been perceived as highly critical – it is difficult to know from the written word alone. A lady asked whether any woman had ever written a great philosophical treatise, any great musical piece, or any great history. Mrs Pankhurst's reply 'ventured to suggest that … as genius was not one of the qualifications for a voter in man, it should not be so in woman.' Another question which was handed in (a sign of timidity?) read: 'Whether it is intended to have universal women's suffrage, and whether women would not ultimately rule the Empire if they increased at the same rate as they do now.' This caused laughter in the hall, but the issue of Empire indicated an argument that was often raised against women's suffrage – that women did not have, and could not obtain, the military or administrative skills which were needed to run the British Empire. Mrs Pankhurst side-stepped that issue and commented instead, not very convincingly, on the fact that more males were born but more females survived and that, if women had the vote, there could be more national mothering for the men.

Mrs Pankhurst's meeting, while attracting great interest and much support immediately, did not have a lasting effect. The branch report in *Votes for Women* (14/07/11) said that they had gained many new members as a result, but these reports were subject to hyperbole as it was also stated that there was a good attendance at the follow-up meeting at Ashley Hall (sic) (21/07/11). This meeting was held in the Apsley Hall the following week, chaired by Ada Flatman, and it was noted by the local press that the attendance was 'rather small'. Again, Miss Flatman referred to the attitude of Colonel Bathurst and suggested that he needed to change it, further provocation to the opponents to which they responded forcefully.

There was also an attempt to rouse Cricklade while Ada Flatman was in the area. She addressed a meeting in the Market Place there on 12 July and, as with the claims about the numbers at Apsley Hall, it was stated that the attendance was good and a successful occasion. Cricklade does not feature again, so one assumes that this was just an isolated event. Although a Cirencester branch of the WSPU was set up, with Mrs Dives as the honorary secretary, while Ada Flatman was in Cornwall during the late summer, little was reported. She returned to whip up support for a visit by Lord Lytton on 9 November while organising a campaign in Stroud too. He was a Conservative peer who stalwartly supported the movement. His sister, Lady Constance Lytton, had acquired fame as the most aristocratic woman to have been imprisoned and subjected to force-feeding. Lord Lytton's appearance may well have been thought of as a counterweight to the Bathurst influence in the town. He was to be accompanied by Mrs Emmeline Pethick-Lawrence, the treasurer of the WSPU, and a very persuasive speaker.

Again, Ada Flatman's organising skill was crucial. She arranged a meeting of 'workers' to give them canvassing literature and Mrs Dives was to organise one half of the district and Miss Grace Hadow the other.[6] This was bolstered by another Market Place meeting and by Mrs Dives recruiting more new members[7]

Poster advertising the WSPU meeting in Cirencester, at which Mrs Pethick-Lawrence was the only eventual speaker because Lord Lytton was unable to come. (Suffragette Fellowship Archive © Museum of London)

Women's Social and Political Union.

NON-PARTY.   FOUNDER: MRS. PANKHURST, 4, CLEMENTS INN, LONDON.

THINK!

Do you really know what Votes for Women means?

READ!

That Women are at last coming into their own and are determined that sex alone shall not be a bar to the rights of Citizenship, realising that they need the protection of the Vote behind their interests in the labour market, exactly as the men do to-day. Women must "work to live," therefore they mean to stand "Women for Women" till the Vote is won.

LEARN!

From **MRS. PETHICK LAWRENCE**, one of the most brilliant orators of our day. She is the Honorary Treasurer of the W.S.P.U., and is also, with her husband, Joint Editor of "Votes for Women." She has spent her life in helping those less fortunate than herself. Known among the poor of London as "Sister Emmeline," and in spite of her noble life she has twice been thrown into prison as a common criminal, being forced to wear the broad arrows and eat prison food that Women may enjoy their political freedom.

KNOW!

From the Right Hon. the **EARL OF LYTTON** the true facts of the Conciliation Bill, which will be introduced next Session. Who so able to explain it as Lord Lytton?—who is the Chairman of the Committee formed to promote the Bill, and who has done such magnificent work in furthering the interests of Women.

Chair: Miss S. ADA FLATMAN.

Bingham Hall, Cirencester
THURSDAY, November 9, at 8.

TICKETS—Numbered and Reserved, 2/6 ; Unreserved, 1/- and 6d.; at Baily and Woods', Market Place.

WILTS & GLOUCESTERSHIRE STANDARD PRINTING WORKS, CIRENCESTER.

(*VFW* 03/11/11). In addition to these efforts, the members, like their fellows in Cheltenham and Stroud, were being urged to make goods for a fundraising Christmas Fair in London, where Gloucestershire members were to supply the woollen stall. (A Miss Henderson was making some lovely gentlemen's waistcoats!) So one suspects that their resources were thinly stretched as, after the 9 November meeting, Cirencester disappears from the branch report section of *Votes for Women*.

---

6   See below for Grace Hadow, more usually labelled a suffragist rather than a suffragette.

7   In late 1911, a donation of 5s was made to national funds by Mrs Smallwood: this was probably Mrs Elizabeth Smallwood of the Ceylon Café in Dyer Street.

The meeting itself was not as planned, as Lord Lytton was not able to come from London. The government had suddenly announced that it was going to introduce a Manhood Suffrage Bill. This would give the vote to all men while slow-pedalling on the proposed vote for women householders, which the Conciliation Bill Committee headed by Lord Lytton was proposing. While this deprived the meeting of its headline speaker, it did enliven it as Mrs Pethick-Lawrence was able to attack the prime minister's action and represent it as a desperate effort by him to avoid demands for women's suffrage. She talked of it as no longer a chess game but now a 'fight', and this is indeed the point at which WSPU tactics escalated. The resolution for the Conciliation Bill proposal was passed by a large majority in the hall after an enthusiastic reception for her speech (*Standard* 10/11/11, *VFW* 17/11/11).

The opposition takes shape

While the WSPU was struggling to make a lasting impact on Cirencester, the opposition forces had been organising. The *Standard* reported that several critical questions were directed at Mrs Pethick-Lawrence and some of the questioners were named. These included Lady Bathurst, and William H. Cole, who had attended the

Pankhurst meeting with his wife and, while admitting that Mrs Pankhurst was impressive, did not agree with her. (He lived at Querns Lane House and his money came through the Wiltshire Bacon Curing Company.) The anti-suffrage campaigners also handed out leaflets as the audience left the hall after the Pethick-Lawrence meeting. They had organised themselves almost immediately after the Pankhurst meeting, and a branch of the National

Mrs Gordon Dugdale of Abbey House, one of the leaders of the Anti-Suffrage Society in Cirencester. (Source unknown)

League for Opposing Woman Suffrage was formed in early August. Countess Bathurst was the president, Mrs Gordon Dugdale of Abbey House the vice president and the host of a meeting in the Abbey Grounds when it was announced that there were already 160 members. That is a very impressive response to the WSPU's arrival in the town and would have presented a formidable opposition. How influential were the Bathursts in national circles?

Ada Flatman had been warned by Christabel Pankhurst of the potential opposition. A letter of 4 July (SF Archive) sent to her at Ashcroft Villas reads: 'Colonel Bathurst will be a difficult man to deal with. Lady Bathurst declines to attend your meeting at Cirencester, but I think we may get her to attend a meeting in London and she may come round as so many anti-suffragists are doing at the moment.'

Christabel Pankhurst's assessment proved to be accurate on him, but not on her! Presumably she was not writing from personal knowledge of either of them. Ada Flatman spoke at a meeting in which she said that she had received a letter from Colonel Bathurst saying that he did not approve of votes for women (*Echo* 17/07/11). She hoped that women would write to him to express their views, but she doubted that he would change his mind as she knew he was going to preside at an anti-suffrage meeting in the near future. She therefore had a very realistic view of the Bathurst opposition.

The National League for Opposing Woman Suffrage took to the Letters section of the *Standard* to try to counter some of the statements made by Ada Flatman. She had apparently been invited to the Abbey Grounds meeting and had been upset by the 'social set' dominating it. In the light of her apparent regard for social status, this is perhaps surprising, but her anger was aroused by feeling slighted. No doubt she had been partly incensed by Colonel Bathurst's speech which suggested that her previous threats of him having to change his mind on women's suffrage were useless: 'He had made up his mind, and he would not alter it in spite of any threat or any flattery … He thought Miss Flatman had better try her energies, her talents, and her oratorical powers on some more plastic material than himself.' Part of her letter demonstrating her distaste for what she encountered read: 'In every district there are those of the cringing type to be found, who will follow anything led by the social set, and those our movement has no use for. All thinking women will look twice before they allow themselves to become a cog on the wheel against the progress of women' (*Standard* 28/06/11). The editorial's response to this was to label her lack of courtesy as 'unpardonable' and accused her of 'vulgar abuse', but she clearly saw the Bathursts and their following as obstructive.

As we have seen, Ada Flatman could be impressed by people of some social standing, so it is interesting that she focused her criticism on the 'social set'. Perhaps

Letters to Miss Flatman from Lord Bathurst and Colonel Ben Bathurst, MP. The appearance of civility masked hostility on both sides. (Suffragette Fellowship Archive © Museum of London)

this was the first instance of a dominant opposing social elite she had met. She kept two letters from the Bathursts in her scrapbook, the first from the current head of the family, the second from Colonel Benjamin Bathurst MP. She presumably regarded them as an important if negative ingredient in her attempt to galvanise Cirencester into action.

Apart from Mrs Ellen Dugdale, the young wife of Major James Gordon Dugdale, other noteworthy leaders of the Anti-Suffrage League included Mrs Martha Leatham of Bagendon Manor, second wife of the former Liberal MP for Huddersfield who was on the magistrates bench with Earl Bathurst and W.H. Cole, and Mr Robert Ellett, a solicitor of Oakley Cottage, Tetbury Road.[8] Mrs Leatham's husband had spoken fiercely against women's suffrage in the Commons on at least one occasion: in 1884, he argued somewhat bitingly that, 'It is not because men

8   What is now McGill Accountants.

pay rates and taxes, or even occupy property, that they have votes but because they are men.'[9] Male opposition of this kind was common and had an effect on many of their women folk.

There is a glimpse of the work of the 'Antis' among the lower classes in Cirencester in a letter from Ada Flatman in the NUWSS paper (*CC* 30/11/11). She, like an earlier correspondent, challenged the report that the Anti-Suffrage League had put out – that they had held a meeting at Mr Boulton's draper's shop in the Market Place[10] and the whole of the staff, apart from ten, had joined. Miss Flatman held a meeting there later and there were protests of indignation at the suggestion of 'Anti' support. About nine young girls 'with their hair down' (implying they were very young) admitted that they had bought buttons but did not realise this committed them to membership and were going to write to the League to withdraw membership.

Ada Flatman and Ethel Colquhoun, from Anti-Suffrage headquarters, exchanged views and 'facts' in the Letters page of the *Standard*, largely based round the economic position of working-class women, until at the beginning of September the editor announced that the correspondence was now closed, under what pressure one can only speculate! Colonel Ben Bathurst took to the Letters page also in early 1912, arguing that women's suffrage had not been an issue when he was elected in December 1910 and should not be so now. Indeed, the whole tone of the paper's coverage had altered with the renewal of WSPU militancy after what was seen as a government betrayal over the Conciliation Bill. 'The hooliganism of the militant section … has aroused a most hostile temper both in and outside the House of Commons' (*Standard* 09/03/12).

However, the press reflected public opinion as much as they steered it. The strength of the 'Antis' was relatively much greater in Cirencester than in Cheltenham, with the physical presence of the Bathursts including a hostile MP, and the local WSPU branch seems to have subsided into silence very quickly. Perhaps the national WSPU campaign, which now included more vicious damage of property through arson, also could not be supported by the Cirencester women.

9 Hansard, HC, Deb., 3rd Series, CCLXXXIX, 12 June 1884, c.102.
10 The business later became Rackhams and then House of Fraser.

The Conservative and Unionist Women's Franchise Association (CUWFA)

Highly significant is the fact that the local honorary secretary of the WSPU, Mrs Dives, who had been so prominent in her support for Mrs Pankhurst's visit, became a leading light in the non-militant Conservative and Unionist Women's Franchise Association when a branch was begun in March 1912. The apparent alienation of some women who believed in the cause but could not support a higher level of militancy may have led to the formation of this non-militant group, which had a quiet strength in Cirencester. The national organiser sent to galvanise Cirencester Conservatives was, like Ada Flatman, aware of the Bathurst obstruction and this is often referred to in the pages of their *Review*. Miss Walford hoped that the WSPU meeting with Lord Lytton would counter some of the anti-suffrage influence, but she wrote that there were 'great difficulties in this place'.

In spite of the 'difficulties', a group was set up with Mrs Laura Swanwick of Coates as the first secretary and, with her committee, she seems to have achieved a growth in membership. She was the wife of Bruce Swanwick, a local farmer and son of Russell Swanwick of College Farm who also had attended the Pankhurst meeting.[11] A considerable coup was that two of the 'principal' doctors of the town and the 'principal' dentist agreed to put the *Review* and the NUWSS *Common Cause* in their waiting rooms, and copies were accepted in the public library. This was a challenge to the 'Antis' and shows that there were some educated professionals who were prepared to oppose them (*CUWFR*, Jan-March and July-September 1912).

The CUWFA did not seek to challenge its fellow societies and there were joint meetings with the local WSS when it was formed. Indeed, when Mrs Swanwick resigned through ill health in early 1913, Grace Hadow of the local WSS took over temporarily, fulfilling a dual role across the two societies. This was not uncommon but suggests a limited pool of committed supporters in the town. The next secretary was Mrs Ethel Zachary, the new wife of the Vicar of Siddington, who was a member of the local wine merchants' family (*CUWFR*, Jan-March 1913). Some CUWFA members joined the NUWSS Pilgrimage in the summer of 1913, but we do not know how far they walked or travelled with it or whether they just provided an audience within the town.

---

11 It seems that the assistant secretary was also from Coates: Miss Gertrude Gibbs, the daughter of the rector.

Unexpectedly in a town like Cirencester, the secretaries' reports suggest that local women were more roused to support the women's cause by meetings on issues such as the white slave traffic (prostitution) and the Sweated Industries. They joined forces with the WSS for three days in autumn 1913 to provide an exhibition and meetings on the Sweated Industries. This seems removed from the majority of the population's experience, but it perhaps provided a welcome contrast to the Bathurst set's complacency.

Cirencester's NUWSS

In July 1912, the WSS newspaper announced the formation of a new branch in Cirencester, its secretary Grace Hadow. The inspiration for this is unclear. The CUWFA preceded it by a few months and, as Grace Hadow was a Conservative, one wonders why she felt that a WSS was necessary. Women taking dual roles was not unknown, but this parallel role so immediately is unusual. She was said to have avoided party politics but, in this period, she was secretary of the Primrose League and was named on the committee of the Conservative and Unionist Association. So one cannot conclude that she had no party allegiance. In the former role, she even had to act alongside Lady Bathurst, who was president: one wonders whether they ever discussed women's suffrage!

Who was Grace Hadow? She was the daughter of a South Cerney vicar and was educated at Truro School in her late teens, where she would have been inspired by a headmistress influenced by Miss Beale of Cheltenham Ladies' College. Earlier, she had experienced some of the frustrations of a very limited education at Brownshill Court near Stroud. She was a very able English student at Oxford and became a tutor at

Miss Grace Hadow, leader of Cirencester suffragists. Brought up in South Cerney, she returned from Oxford to Cirencester to look after her mother. (*Wiltshire and Glos Standard*, 3 September 2015)

Lady Margaret Hall there. It was at Oxford that her interest in women's suffrage developed, but her mother and brother were both 'Antis' and her brother made her promise not to get involved. However, she soon asked to be released from that promise.

By now, her mother was widowed and in poor health. She lived at Foss Lodge, Sheep Street, in Cirencester. In 1909, Grace began to care for her mother and only travelled weekly to Oxford, eventually resigning her post, but remaining as a visiting lecturer. As her older sister Constance was living at home already, it is not clear why this happened or what pressure was put on her[12] – for she did not particularly like the atmosphere in Cirencester. She felt it was a cultural desert – 'brains were disliked, especially in women' – and that women's suffrage was not a hopeful cause. She will have seen Miss Flatman's efforts to establish a WSPU hit the Bathurst train, and yet a year later she was working with the CUWFA and the WSS.

Grace Hadow did not enjoy the canvassing in the backyards behind the streets, nor the sparse village meetings, and she may well have seemed 'donnish and critical' according to her biographer. She also felt that she earned 'unpopularity with the local great' but, as shown above, she worked with Lady Bathurst in the Primrose League. It is more interesting to speculate how she tolerated this! She also is found giving a hearty vote of thanks to the other instigator of the League for Opposing Women's Suffrage, Mrs Ellen Dugdale of Abbey House. This was at a meeting to hear about the operation of the Poor Law, when Mrs Dugdale suggested her sister Miss Constance Hadow be nominated for election as Poor Law Guardian. Constance's work in South Cerney and her work visiting the workhouse in Cirencester were both commended (*Standard* 17/01/14). So, although she attended the post-Pankhurst meeting in 1911, Constance Hadow's contribution to women's greater involvement was social, whereas Grace's was political.

Records of what the WSS achieved in Cirencester are very slight. Joint meetings with the CUWFA on the white slave traffic (prostitution) and on organising an exhibition on the 'Sweated Industries' were held, a sensible joining of resources, especially as many women had dual membership, not least Grace Hadow! There was an emphasis on targeting lower-class women or their champions: in addition to the above, the January 1913 AGM was addressed by Mr Baillie Weaver from London, who showed how women were disadvantaged in the labour market. She

---

12 However, a diary entry when she was 15 declared that 'I will always do what she (her mother) wishes, she bears so much for us' (H. Deneke: *Grace Hadow*). Her mother had certainly been the pivot of parish and family life in South Cerney.

brought Mrs Haverfield from Oxford to address the 1914 AGM; she spoke not only about the history of the movement, but also about the problems of infant mortality and bad housing. At the same meeting, her friend and future biographer, Helena Deneke, with her sister Margaret, manned the literature stall at the fundraising White Elephant Sale (which brought in a noteworthy £15): they were visiting from Oxford. And the ubiquitous Dr Alice Burn and Flora Kelley from Cheltenham performed their *Mrs Chicky* party piece.

By this time, the president was Mrs Percival, the widow of a retired major-general, from Daglingworth House. Also in the CUWFA, together with Mrs Zachary, she gave the WSS a very sedate tone. Mrs Mary Kitson, another stallholder at the sale, was the wife of the Vicar of Watermoor. Grace Hadow's speech at the sale urged women to join the Friends of Women's Suffrage scheme as a way of showing Asquith and the government the extent of support for the cause. Whether her audience included members of the lower classes we cannot know, but this scheme had been begun by the NUWSS to attract women who could not afford membership but were prepared to sign a card of support. There are reports of how many Friends cards were signed, for example eight on one day in November. Her claim that the district could now claim over 200 prepared to form a suffrage society sounds excessive, but her claim at the next meeting that the membership doubled in a year after the outrages against them in 1913, described below, sounds realistic.

Miss Hadow's own efforts were more dispersed by then. Working for the West of England Federation, she visited places such as Nailsworth, Chipping Campden and Welford-on-Avon to help found branches. A meeting was held at Fairford in May 1913 to try to 'break new ground' but, as with the WSPU earlier, there was no permanent impact. This was perhaps because the 'Antis' had been there immediately beforehand at the infant school so the WSS was refused that venue and had to meet at the Bull Inn (*CC* 30/05/13).

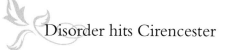# Disorder hits Cirencester

The WSS Pilgrimage to London in 1913 had encountered vicious attacks in Cheltenham on 15 July, as we have seen, and the pilgrims suffered a similar fate in Cirencester the next day. Miss Grace Hadow had organised a meeting in the Market Place to greet the Cheltenham contingent, and some local members had met them outside the town to escort them. The Principal of the Agricultural College, Professor Ainsworth-Davis, had been concerned that some of his students might cause trouble and had warned them against such behaviour. Apparently, he was ignored.

About fifteen to twenty ladies arrived in total, and Mrs Swiney 'and friends' (one of whom was Dr Alice Burn), in the colours of red, green and white, arrived in a brake and pair and positioned themselves in front of the church and Town Hall. One report suggested a crowd of 3,000 to 5,000 had gathered, but the size of the marketplace and of the town suggests this was an exaggeration. As soon as the chairman, Mr J.W. Ainsworth of Swindon, had made opening remarks emphasising that they were the law-abiding section of the movement, 'there was a chorus of shrieks, whistling and booing, which was followed by the arrival on the scene of a band of eleven players in a motor-car, which included some young men wearing masks and attired in fancy costumes … the arrival of this band was the signal for much jostling and free fights in all directions' (*Chronicle* 19/07/13). Even though Mr Ainsworth, an auctioneer, was used to a lively audience, his appeals for calm were ignored. It seems that the young men in the car were students but many more in the crowd were out for trouble. Miss Hadow and Mrs Swiney both tried to speak – with no effect. Local members Mr and Mrs Dives and Mr Connal,[13] all previously of the WSPU, were there and took refuge in the brake as rotten fruit, eggs and vegetables were thrown. Some women ran to the police station for protection and PC Holland saved one woman from being killed, according to her.

As in Cheltenham, it was decided to end the meeting. They tried to move to Watermoor to continue, so the brake went via Dyer Street and Victoria Road – but was followed by crowds, some on bicycles and the young men in the motor car. So the driver diverted towards Chesterton but, at the canal bridge, the crowd attempted to tip the brake into the canal. Driving towards Siddington, some young men seized the horses' heads but the driver used his whip on them. Finding themselves down a dead-end lane, they took refuge in a cottage (or cottages, depending on which report is used). The Siddington cottagers were more respectful than the crowds remaining in the marketplace, who hounded any women in suffrage colours and generally caused mayhem.

Those besieged in Siddington were soon given protection by two policemen, and at 11.30 p.m. it was decided it was safe to leave, another police sergeant following the brake on a bicycle. The reporter from the *Chronicle* was with him and witnessed how he outwitted some young men on bicycles, causing them to run in the opposite direction. The reporter had also spoken to Mrs Swiney who 'spoke in high praise of the conduct of the police, the driver of the brake, and scores of working men who did all they could to protect the Suffragists from violence'.

---

13 A civil engineer of 19 Ashcroft Villas.

Her praise is interesting in light of the fact that a question was asked in Parliament about the response of the police to 'serious' assaults on the women at St Neot's, Stafford, Tiverton and Cirencester. Cirencester had been singled out with only three other places to ask the Home Secretary why no arrests had been made – as events seem to have been little worse than at Cheltenham, one wonders whether these were sample cases or whether particular complaints had been made (*Hansard Debate* 13 August 1913).

Things were no better at Swindon, where Miss Mills of Cheltenham was speaking from a carriage when it was rushed by the crowd and she had to take refuge in the post office. On this occasion, there was a greater police presence and they managed to take Miss Mills and her fellow speaker to safety in a tramcar.

Little is said about the local Cirencester participants, but Miss Hadow later said that she had only been mobbed once in her campaigning, so this would have been the occasion. It is unclear whether any Cirencester members went to Swindon or beyond. If the occasion did cause outraged sympathisers to join the WSS, as Grace Hadow claimed, then it had a positive effect. It is impossible to know how far this is true, or whether an increased membership would have remained as the outbreak of war caused splintering in the movement. One suspects that the Bathurst factor in the town would ultimately have proved decisive.

STROUD: TWO MEN LEAD THE WAY

After Stroud's relatively good response to the 1866 petition (see Chapter 2), we might expect a vigorous group to have emerged – but that does not seem to have been the case. A short-lived group was set up in 1871 but, as in many other areas, nothing more is heard after 1873. Even in the early years of the twentieth century, after the formation of the NUWSS with branches all over the country, nothing seems to have stirred in Stroud. Radicalism was of the pro-Liberal kind, so any anti-Liberal suffragist agitation after the formation of the 1905 Liberal government was difficult. Moreover, the Liberal MP from 1900, Charles Allen, was not in favour of women's suffrage. The *Stroud Journal* was rabidly pro-Liberal with a strength of partisanship not found in the Cheltenham press, for example, while *Stroud News* was pro-Conservative, but a little less forceful in tone. How far the papers reflected or influenced local opinion cannot be known, but the party rivalry did not help the suffrage cause.

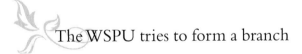

The WSPU tries to form a branch

The first positive move was made in 1911 by the WSPU. This was the result of Miss Ada Flatman, the WSPU organiser in the county, moving on to Stroud after her efforts in Cheltenham and Cirencester. As far as we know, she was not responding to any request from local sympathisers. She reported to *Votes for Women* with her usual optimism that she intended to 'open up Stroud' and that it promised to be 'a good centre' (*VFW* 08/09/11).

Perhaps the difficulty of moving around to drum up enough support, however, was recognised by her request for the loan of a bicycle as there are 'no trains'.[1] One

---

1   Not true in the absolute sense but true in terms of reaching outlying areas.

can see in the first planned meetings that she saw the need to draw on outlying areas, as she arranged an At Home in Painswick, a meeting at the Painswick Institute, another at the Stonehouse Subscription Rooms and the major one at the Holloway Institute, Stroud. Very soon there was another at the Chalford National Schools. The first was based on the support of Mrs Clara Herbert and her daughter Mrs Caroline Sandford, who lived at Paradise House, Painswick. Her husband was a solicitor living in London during the week with her son-in-law, a barrister. She and her daughter were prepared to open their home and to donate considerable sums of money to the cause. No account of the Painswick Institute or Stonehouse meetings survive, so we do not know whether they were successful. The required optimism led to Miss Flatman's statement that all meetings went well!

The meeting at the Holloway Institute was deemed a success in both the *Stroud Journal* and other Gloucestershire papers. There was a good attendance and no dissent to the motion that women who were already municipal voters should have the parliamentary vote, and that Mr Allen, the MP, should not obstruct any bill to this effect. Unanimity was achieved in spite of the mixed audience of Conservatives and Liberals, and the *Journal* did not yet attack the cause. The cross-party feeling was reinforced by the fact that the chairman was Mr Frank Gwynne Evans, the leading Liberal in the area, and that he was supported by Miss Gladys Seymour Keay, of the Women's Liberal Association and Mrs E.H. Hawkins, the wife of Rev. Edward Hawkins, vicar of Holy Trinity Church and a fervent Conservative. Although the press, particularly the *Journal*, tried to talk up a personal party rivalry between Mr Gwynne Evans and Rev. Hawkins as damaging to the women's suffrage cause, in fact they co-operated on the issue. Mr Frank Gwynne Evans was a retired barrister, though only in his thirties, living with his wife and two servants at Tower House, Woodchester. His leisured existence allowed him to devote much time to local Liberalism – but also to women's suffrage when the issue arose.

The speaker at the Holloway Institute meeting was Miss Evelyn Sharp, the writer and journalist who had visited Cheltenham earlier in the year

Mr Frank Gwynne Evans, leading Stroud Liberal and supporter of women's suffrage. (*Stroud Journal*, 9 August 1912)

Mr F. Gwynne Evans.

and who was about to become actively militant in joining in window-breaking. Her speech is given little coverage, but more is given to Mr Evans, who seemed to emphasise the need for women to vote because of their special concern for children, the sick and the suffering, as well as the morals of the country. This 'women's sphere' argument would not have appealed to all women but was frequently used. A more fiery speech was delivered by the young Mr Frederick Wake, who was a provision assistant in a grocery business at the time. His job may have given him some insight into the lives of working women, as he gave an impassioned plea for consideration of women who had to work in factories to support their families, although the proposed bill would not have actually given them the vote. Mr Wake later became president of the local Trades and Labour Council, clearly a young man with a social conscience.

Miss Flatman was lodging at Oak Villa, Stratford Road, with Mrs Emily Birt, a widow, living with her farmer son-in-law and daughter. She acquired a number of helpers, particularly Miss Gladys Seymour Keay, a young woman from a wealthy banking family based in both Minchinhampton and Kensington. She and her sister both contributed rather small amounts to WSPU funds, but she was obviously keen to help by assisting in publicising meetings and chairing the one at Chalford. Mr Gwynne Evans eventually chaired it but she did speak at the meeting. Another Minchinhampton woman who, with her husband, gave support and opened her house for an At Home meeting, was Mrs Mary Church of The Coign. Her husband, a surgeon, was a very active and respected member of the community, as was demonstrated by the tributes to him when they left for Canada in March 1913. Other women helped by canvassing, among them Mrs Gwynne Evans. A valuable donor at this time, and a neighbour of the Gwynne Evans, was Mr Henry Workman of Woodchester Lodge, a wealthy timber merchant, who gave 18s 6d to WSPU funds.

Ada Flatman kept a cutting about a debate in Brimscombe in her scrapbook, which briefly described the Wesley Guild's debate on women's suffrage conducted as far as possible on the lines of a full-dress Commons debate, complete with a gilded mace laid on the table! It was a vigorous debate with the motion only carried by thirty-one to twenty-four votes (SF Archive). A meeting with Annie Kenney as speaker was advertised for 23 November, an event for which there might have been much local interest from the millworkers in hearing a fellow-worker. However, Miss Flatman left no cutting about it, nor is there any press report of the meeting, so one presumes it was cancelled, probably as the result of the repercussions of the mass window-breaking in London's West End on 21 November in which Annie Kenney was involved.

In the meantime, just as in Cheltenham and Cirencester, members seem to have been embroiled in the making of things for the woollen stall for which the Gloucestershire groups were responsible. An appeal for badly-needed dress materials, dressing gowns, dressing jackets and jersey was made, and individuals were singled out for praise – Mrs Eliza Green of Prospect House, Cairnscross Road, the comfortably-off widow of a clergyman, was thanked for her woollen cape and a girl's 'tam o'shanter', and a Miss Whittaker made three dressing gowns. Tweeds made at Stroud Cloth Mills were to be a special feature of the stall.

While all this fairly low-key endeavour was going on, the *Journal* was attacking the women's suffrage efforts with considerable invective. It praised Asquith's goodwill and condemned the 'childish folly' of the suffragettes, but did grudgingly admit the need to 'follow our Colonies' and give women the vote.

Unfortunately, just as with the Annie Kenney meeting, Mrs Pankhurst's advertised meeting for 29 February 1912 was cancelled – or, at least, she was unable to come because of illness, but Lady Constance Lytton was drafted in. As we have seen, Lady Constance was a doughty fighter who was 'four times a gaolbird and three times a stone-thrower' (*Journal*, 01/03/12) who been subjected to forcible feeding. But she remained a Tory aristocrat, and there may not have been many in Stroud who would have welcomed that, although Miss Flatman would, as we have seen in Cheltenham. Also in the chair was Lady Isabel Margesson of Barnt Green, Worcestershire, whose daughter, Catherine, had been imprisoned and was a WSPU organiser in Reading. Both ladies were prepared to defend stone-throwing as justified militancy. A heckler from the floor so annoyed Miss Flatman that she said she too was going to London and 'intended to smash some property in order to draw attention to the way women had been treated'. She observed that it was the men at the back of the hall who had not paid for their seats who were being disruptive, a sign that she was rattled by the response.

Announcement of Mrs Pankhurst's meeting in Stroud which she then cancelled. (*Stroud Journal*, 2 February 1912)

SUBSCRIPTION ROOMS, STROUD

THURSDAY, FEB. 29th, at 8.

MRS.

PANKHURST

CHAIR :

THE LADY ISABEL MARGESSON

Tickets at Burr's Music Shop, George Street.
Reserved Seats 2/6.   Unreserved 1/-, and 6d.

The repercussions from this meeting were fought out in the hostile press. 'Jonathan', the editorial commentator in the *Journal*, felt, understandably because of Lady Lytton's presence, that the meeting had been a Tory one. He doubted whether Mrs Pankhurst had really been too ill to come to Stroud and suspected that she was merely preparing for another window-smashing escapade. The next day there had been attacks on windows in Bond Street and Oxford Street with toffee-hammers(!), and on 4 March on government offices:

> The most perfect mechanism will sometimes go wrong and in that case we can only suppose like the old war-horse the sound of the trumpet proved too captivating, and copying David of old, she armed herself with pebbles, and put herself in the front line of battle … At present, the violent Amazons of the movement have undoubtedly set the current flowing strongly against votes for women.
>
> (*Journal* 08/03/12)

A poem was also published, 'The Biter Bit (Dedicated to Miss F★L★T★M★N)', describing the pursuit of a woman who has tried to hammer shopfronts and ending:

> The world endures its harmless cranks,
> But draws the line at lawless stuff.

Miss Flatman's poetic retort the next week, headed 'The Bitten Bites', stated that peaceful campaigning had been unsuccessful, and women had to fight for 'Freedom':

> Man the omnipotent law-maker
> Drives every woman to be a law-breaker.

The *Journal* did not give up – in April it published a supposedly humorous dialogue between a husband and wife where the husband, Jasper Jenkins, defends the women and the wife, Jasmine Jenkins, condemns their use of ''ammers and stwuns and 'oss-whips' to make their point.

References to the WSPU in Stroud disappear after this – although it is possible that meetings occurred. This is unlikely as the WSPU's own newspaper (by now *The Suffragette* after a split between the Pankhursts and the Pethick-Lawrences, who retained the title *Votes for Women*) did not refer to Stroud again. Also, the *News* published letters to the editor condemning militancy in 1912, in a lengthy exchange going on for two months without any local references at all. One of

Letters to the Editor.

The Editor does not hold himself responsible for opinions expressed by correspondents

THE SUFFRAGIST CRIMINALS.

Sir.—If Mr. K. Douglas Smith, in his gallant but rather hopeless attempt to defend the Suffragist conspirators, had confined himself to matters of opinion, no rejoinder from me would have been necessary. Your readers can decide for themselves whether, for instance, I am right or wrong in thinking that no motive whatsoever could possibly justify or extenuate deliberate and carefully prepared acts of hooliganism in our public thoroughfares; and whether women guilty of such criminal conduct can truly be said to be possessed of "personal integrity and a desire for right and justice." Again, it may be my own crass stupidity which prevents me from seeing the smallest analogy between the "Jameson Raid"—that gallant but unfortunate blunder in South African history—and a mere vulgar conspiracy to commit wholesale damage to shop windows in the principal streets of London, regardless even of whether the shopkeepers were for or against woman's suffrage. Mr. Smith's letter will undoubtedly be in harmony with the views of everyone who is opposed to the repression of organised lawlessness and ruffianism.

MISS WHEELER.

A verbal attack on the suffragettes, alongside a picture and account of the wedding of one of them (albeit unknown to the editor) to a Stroud clergyman! (*Stroud News*, 21 June 1912)

these, headed 'The Suffragist Criminals', was published alongside a long account of the wedding of Rev. Beauvais of Whitehills to Miss Eira Wheeler of Cheltenham. The irony of this is that she was an active member of Cheltenham WSPU before her marriage (see Cheltenham WSPU chapter). So it seems that WSPU activity in Stroud disappeared without a branch ever having been formed.

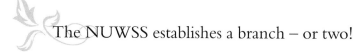

The NUWSS establishes a branch – or two!

However, perhaps the cause had not died. A report in *The Common Cause*, the NUWSS newspaper, said in November 1912 that Stroud was simply 'asking' for suffrage! The only evidence of this is a debate earlier that month at the Stroud

National Union of Women's Suffrage Societies.

NON-MILITANT.

PRESIDENT : MRS. HENRY FAWCETT, L.L.D.

A PUBLIC MEETING

under the auspices of the above Society
will be held in

THE HOLLOWAY INSTITUTE,

On Thursday, November 28th,

AT 8 P.M.

Advertisement for the arrival of the NUWSS in Stroud. The meeting was chaired by the Tory Rev. Edward Hawkins of Holy Trinity Church. (*Stroud Journal*, 22 November 1912)

Literary and Debating Society, with an invitation to the Conservative Debating Society. The motion was 'That Woman's Suffrage is Desirable' (*News* 08/11/12). A full account of the meeting shows that men argued equally vigorously on both sides, exploring the history of the movement, women's mental fitness to vote, the examples of Australia and New Zealand, whether women wanted the vote and their role in the home. Mr Gwynne Evans made his usual intervention in favour, relating his points to the struggle of women to earn 'her daily bread' since the Industrial Revolution.

As the meeting was split in its views, it was hardly compelling evidence of Stroud's desire for another women's suffrage society. However, two women, Miss Blackstone of Bath and Miss Coyle from Essex were working in Tewkesbury and Stroud with the intention of founding branches. A meeting was advertised for 28 November at the Holloway Institute, and Miss Coyle spoke at Stroud Ethical Church on the same day.

The meeting at the Holloway Institute was not a success: there was a low attendance, attributed by the reporter to 'many other fixtures in town and country'. Nothing of great attraction appears to have been advertised unless everyone had decamped to the Newbury Races or a Red Cross Entertainment in Nailsworth! The speakers were not national figures, so would not have been a great draw: after Rev. Hawkins' speech, Dr Elizabeth Sloan Chesser spoke. She was an interesting woman: qualified as a doctor in her native Glasgow in 1901, she had married and was currently working as a medical journalist. She wrote books on the health of children, motherhood and sex education and was attracted by the idea of eugenics and the improvement of the race through the role of women.[2] As she lived at

---

2   A cause also supported by Dr Burn in Cheltenham, for example.

Churcham, just outside Gloucester, where her husband was farming, she was able to talk to women's suffrage groups in the area, but perhaps would not have had the appeal of some national personalities. More relevant is the observation by 'Jonathan's Jottings' in the *Journal* that the meeting was held in the Tory Holloway Institute and chaired by the Conservative Rev. Hawkins: he felt that the strongly party-political venue would have been off-putting to many. As before, 'Jonathan' perceived the Liberal Mr Gwynne Evans as an opponent of Rev. Hawkins, but he was in the audience and Miss Seymour Keay, also a Liberal, seconded his vote of thanks. What 'Jonathan' does not take into account is that, early in 1912, the NUWSS had formed an electoral alliance with Labour which both the two major parties would have disliked, so perhaps they had more in common than not.

Rev. Hawkins expressed his views in a lively and amusing way, while acknowledging the presence of his 'friend Mr Gwynne Evans':

> What nonsense it was to say that the women ought to stay at home, when they were already engaged in so many spheres of useful political activity. What did the men do who used this argument? They had their mixed foresomes (sic) at golf and bridge. They had their mixed foresomes (sic) at croquet and lawn tennis, and there were other things in which men and women were equally interested.
>
> (*Journal* 29/11/12)

What is interesting is that all the key figures in the earlier WSPU meetings were here again to try to launch the WSS in the town. Was that because they had been disillusioned by the WSPU's escalation of militancy? Rev. Hawkins certainly thought so, condemning any action leading to destruction of property. Or were they keen to support a women's suffrage branch of any complexion?

Dr Elizabeth Sloan Chesser of Churcham, Gloucestershire, a doctor and writer on women's and children's health, who spoke at Stroud and other WSS societies. (Freepages.genealogy. rootsweb/ancestry.com. Owner unknown)

In spite of lukewarm support from the town, a branch was formed as a result of this initiative. The first meeting was held at Upland House by permission of Mrs Wilkins, when nine local members elected a committee. Again, the same names appear with Rev. Hawkins elected chairman and Mr Gwynne Evans treasurer. It is unusual for a branch to be so dominated by two men, rather than women taking at least one of the key roles. Mrs Mills of Lower Street was secretary and a committee of five women was elected, including Miss Seymour Keay of Minchinhampton and two men.

A year later, a meeting of the branch was held at the Corn Hall (*Stroud News* 14/11/13). Again, a small attendance was noted so the branch was not thriving. The honorary secretary was Miss Nancie Gorton of London Road. Two other women on the committee were Mrs Hardy, wife of Dr Henry Hardy, and Miss Fanny Blake who was a head teacher, living in Middle Street, Uplands, with her widowed mother. Two men were on the committee, Mr William Knight of Rodborough Common who was a retired corn merchant, and the young Labour activist Mr Frederick Wake, who had supported the women's movement when the WSPU arrived in town. A visiting speaker, Miss Meikle, tried to urge the branch to more action and suggested that the movement would bring class unity. Like Dr Sloan Chesser the previous year, she emphasised the suffering of working women 'working and living under conditions which prevented them being adequately fed, housed or clothed'. This would have resonance in a town with so many working women.

The theme was pursued in a meeting held in March 1914, when Miss Grace Hadow from Cirencester spoke of the need for women's political participation in order to address the issue of sweated labour among women. 'It might be the expensive Court shoes which were shod the feet of a queen, or cheap tailored goods, which were produced under sweated conditions' (*Journal* 06/03/14). The vote would give women the power to reform these conditions.

While the Stroud society may have been struggling to gain numbers in the town, a meeting held in Amberley School Room in January 1914 suggesting the geographical spread of the society, reflected in the homes of the above committee members. Four new members joined at the meeting. Overall, the society seemed to be growing and the affiliation fee doubled between 1913 and 1914, suggesting a doubling of membership, but there is no evidence of women of the lower classes to whom they had appealed.

However, a branch was formed in Nailsworth in early 1914, which would take members from Stroud. At the 'kind invitation of Miss Clissold and Mrs Meredith' a successful meeting was held at the Subscription Rooms with a 'gratifying' attendance. Miss Clissold was probably one of the two unmarried daughters in their thirties of Mr William Clissold, retired brewer of Chestnut Hill. Mrs Mary

Meredith was the wife in her fifties of a law clerk, living at Woodlands in the town. Presumably, they would have issued invitations and borne the cost of the rooms, the tea and the speaker's expenses. The outside speaker was Miss Geraldine Cooke, who gave a stirring address, exhorting them to support a movement which would move women to a higher level, working with men for the good of the state as a whole. Then the sexes could be recognised as complementary and equal (*Journal* 23/01/14). The chair was taken by Mrs Walton of Horsley Priory (wife of a retired wire cord manufacturer). She made a speech in which she said that women had long been interested in the subject, as Disraeli had shown in his novel *Sybil*.[3] Miss Clissold urged more women to work on public bodies (as a Poor Law Guardian, for example) as preparation for the parliamentary vote.

The nature of the speeches does not suggest that working women were much in evidence. What happened afterwards supports that. There was a meeting of local members after the main meeting, and Miss Meade-King of Dunkirk Manor House, Amberley, was appointed secretary and Miss Blacke of Nailsworth treasurer (*CC* 24/04/14). In the summer, Mrs Walton entertained the society in her garden, with over sixty attending, and Miss Hadow from Cirencester spoke. Although she spoke about the need for more women to have a voice in questions such as housing and women's sweated labour, she acknowledged the genteel nature of the audience by talking more about the question of Empire. The Rector of Amberley, Rev. Warner, followed her: the Church should support the movement – Christ had rebuked Martha for paying too much attention to her household duties rather than having wider interests! The afternoon was successful in gaining two new members and ten 'Friends', who signed cards of support (*CC* 26/06/14 and *Journal* 26/06/14). This society had little time to get established before the outbreak of war, and its initial affiliation fee suggests only a handful of members – but it had some influential supporters.[4]

Was women's suffrage a failure in the Stroud area?

The impression gained from reading the local newspapers is that women's suffrage was just not a major issue. In the period when the WSPU tried its luck, the chief topic of letters and articles was the Insurance Bill, which would have implications for existing

---

3   Both the Merediths and the Waltons were involved in the local Conservative Party.
4   Another wealthy and influential supporter was Miss Emily Vere Annesley of Barns Close, Amberley. She seconded the vote of thanks at the Garden Party.

Should Ladies Vote?

This is a question of which we have heard much recently, and which is likely to be very much in the fore in the near future.

There may be two opinions as to the wisdom of entrusting LADIES with a Vote for Parliament, but there can be only one as to the advisability of giving them the CASTING VOTE to decide when and by whom the cellar shall be filled with COAL.

Their vote and interest are hereby solicited, with the advice to keep the cellar well filled this Winter as prices are advancing and likely to continue doing so.

Address:

C. W. JONES,
NAILSWORTH.

Telephone No. 311.

Truck Loads to any Stations in
— England at Colliery Prices. —

An advertisement for coal, using women's suffrage as a 'peg'. (*Stroud Journal*, 22 November 1912)

schemes in the town. Irish Home Rule and Welsh Disestablishment (of the Church) also raised great concern over the period. Perhaps the true colours of Stroud are seen in the many column inches about vegetarianism, which does not seem to have been linked to the women's movement as it was in Cheltenham. One must also not forget the very acute local issue which affected women but did not seem to translate into suffragism. Many women worked at the cloth mills and in 1913 there was a strike, centred on the inequality of pay and the right to join a union. The women's suffrage speakers do not seem to have addressed this kind of issue in the town, so could be seen to be out of touch. The more 'leisured' society of Nailsworth, with its associated places such as Amberley and Horsley, may have eventually proved more successful. Even a Nailsworth coal merchant felt that it was worth tapping into the interest in the subject in his advert! He must have felt that it would strike a chord in the minds of some prospective customers!

12

'THE BOOK OF REVELATION' – WHO SUPPORTED THE MOVEMENT?

The discovery in the Gloucestershire Archives of this book of nearly 500 signatures was one of which every researcher dreams! It is a book of signatures presented to the Cheltenham MP Sir James Agg-Gardner in 1912, to thank him for his support for women's suffrage.

The study of the women's suffrage movement in the years before the First World War has been dogged by the fact that, on the whole, no branch minutes or membership lists remain, particularly for the WSPU, who were worried that their activities and members could be identified by the authorities. Absolutely nothing remains for this area and one is forced to look at the local and national suffrage newspapers to glean names. These tend to identify the leaders, but not the names of

Frontispiece of book of thanks to James Agg-Gardner, MP for introducing the second reading of the Conciliation Bill in 1912. Although unsuccessful, his efforts were much appreciated in Cheltenham and the wider area. (D5130/6/6 by kind permission Gloucestershire Archives)

women who perhaps worked tirelessly in the background, or who sold papers on the streets, or who attended meetings and gave small or large amounts of money. The amazing contribution of this book is that it does begin to reveal some of these women – and more male supporters. Because initials or Christian names are given, cross-referencing to the 1911 census can reveal details of age, address, occupation and family structure to put flesh on the bones of what would otherwise just be a name.

Why was the book compiled?

On 28 March 1912, the Conservative MP for Cheltenham, James Agg-Gardner, was centre stage in the House of Commons. He was introducing the second reading of the Conciliation Bill which proposed to give the vote to about 1 million women.[1] This bill was supported by both suffragists and suffragettes but circumstances dictated that it would fail. This was due to a number of factors. Firstly, more Liberals were now in favour of a wider bill which would enfranchise more women who would, they thought, vote Liberal, whereas they were concerned that a narrower female franchise would favour the Conservatives. Secondly, those MPs who were wavering were likely to be put off by the renewed WSPU violence of window-breaking and attacks on property. There were 190 arrests at the beginning of March after attacks on the shop windows in the West End, police raided WSPU headquarters, Christabel Pankhurst had escaped to France and was being sought, while Emmeline Pankhurst was released from Holloway on the day of the debate. And thirdly, the Irish Nationalist members voted against the bill because they did not want to risk losing Asquith's support for a Home Rule Bill. So, the women had partly damaged their own cause, but were also the victims of party politics. 'The window-smashers have smashed themselves' announced the *Pall Mall Gazette*. The bill was defeated by just fourteen votes.

In spite of the defeat, Agg-Gardner was hailed as a hero by the women's movement in Cheltenham. The CUWFA therefore organised a presentation to him of a book of thanks, signed by their members, in co-operation with the WSS and WFL. It was presented to Agg-Gardner at a joint meeting on 12 April. A section of the book had also been opened to 'Sympathisers' as so many, other than members of the three societies, had wanted to sign. He had been unhappy that his bill might

---

1   It was essentially the same bill which had been passed by the Commons in 1911, but was then not given parliamentary time to go any further.

have failed because of a revulsion at militant activity, but the Cheltenham WSPU were completely untouched by the actions of their London colleagues and many of them therefore were amongst those who signed the book as 'Sympathisers'.

There are questions about this book yet unanswered. It only took about a fortnight to collect the signatures, so the organisation must have been very slick and the response enthusiastic. Did people have to come to a central point to sign it? Was it taken round to various focal points in the town? Were some people requested to sign it? How were some people from well outside the area able to sign?

The Women's Freedom League – This find provides a wealth of information, apart from the excitement for a researcher of seeing the signatures of all the key women in one place and imagining how they may have congregated to sign. It gives some idea of the relative strength of the three named groups. For example, the WFL appears to have collected only nineteen local names out of forty-one in total, which rather reinforces the view already formed that they were a small, closely-knit and determined group. Most of the signatories are the women who can be identified as activists from newspaper accounts, but there were also signatures from a number of national figures who were visiting the town, as well as some from the Bristol area.

Equally, the **Women's Suffrage Society**, which has been seen to have struggled to gain support in the early years of the century, appears not to have gained a huge

Signatures of the key WFL Cheltenham personalities. (D5130/6/6 by kind permission Gloucestershire Archives)

195

following. Forty-seven names are on their list, of whom we can identify forty-one. The list is interesting because, while there are many of the names which had represented the society over a number of years, such as Mrs Swiney, Mrs and Miss Mills, with a letter from Dr Callaway asking to be included, there is not the heavy ex-military/colonial presence of earlier. Instead, some of that group, such as Colonel and Mrs Rogers of Battledown Court, signed under the CUWFA banner. It was perfectly possible to be members of more than one society, but it is significant that some chose to be recognised as CUWFA supporters, indicating their party allegiance to Agg-Gardner. Miss Emily Platt, the early WSS secretary who was secretary of the Primrose League, is an obvious example, but Dr Eveline Cargill, who had been on the WSS committee more recently, also made that choice, as did her partner Dr Beatrice Harrison, and Dr Grace Stewart Billings.

Ex-colonial wealth is still evident, but there is a little more commercial representation. For example, Mary Jordan, the wife of a coal merchant of 8 Royal Parade, together with her two daughters Mary and Helen, were signatories, as was Mrs Kate Jackson, of 41 Clarence Square, wife of a grocer. More interesting is the presence of Edith and Emmie Holloway, who may well also have evaded the census.

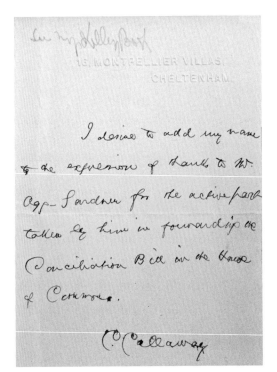

Letter from Dr Charles Callaway, long-time WSS supporter, asking to be included in the book. (D5130/6/6 by kind permission Gloucestershire Archives)

Trade-card of the firm of photographers, Holloway, whose daughters, Edith and Emmie, supported women's suffrage,. Emmie often performed at WSS socials. (www.photohistory-sussex. co.uk)

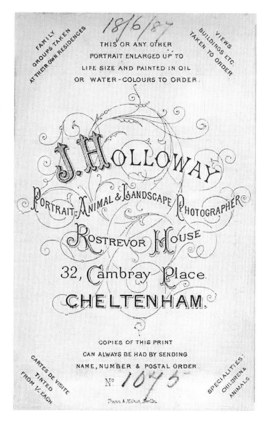

Edith (Bertha) had taken over her father's photography business in Cambray Place in the early years of the century and her sister Elizabeth assisted. This was a family where women were accepted as professional photographers, as Mr Jesse Holloway had previously worked in partnership with his sister, Mrs Jane Beard, who also moved to Cheltenham. Women of independence and talent such as these were likely to be supporters.

In contrast with the other two societies, the **Conservative and Unionist Women's Franchise Association** appears to have gained a large membership within a few years of existence and to have been able to attract more people from lower down the social scale. The book was signed by 131 people, three times the number for both the WFL and WSS. One must be aware, however, that the acclaim was being given to their Conservative MP and some may have been driven by their party allegiance rather than by their feminism. That may also be true of the numbers of Conservative men found under the Sympathisers heading.

Again, there are the names one would expect such as Flora Kelley, the secretary, together with her sisters, Angel and Maud, and her mother Rose. However, there is also Mrs Frances Stirling, who had been an avid WSPU supporter, who had written her protest on the census form. Miss Constance Andrews, one of the three sisters who had taught at CLC, and whose house was used for WSPU meetings while her sister Miss Ellen Andrews was local secretary, signed as a CUWFA supporter. It was often said that the Pankhursts, particularly Christabel, inclined to the Conservatives in these later years in spite of their early ILP links, but one cannot draw the same conclusion from the few Cheltenham examples. In fact, more known WSPU supporters such as Miss Ellen Andrews and her sister Alice, and Mrs Constance Ferguson and Miss Gertrude Blandford, who had also acted as secretary, and Miss Eira Wheeler who collected the woollen goods, signed as Sympathisers.

There is a smattering of less well-heeled members, such as Mr and Mrs Henry Granville who had a second-hand furniture shop in Upper Bath Road, but many of those listed were living in great comfort, such as Miss Mary Fenton, a single lady in her mid-thirties who was living with her widowed mother and six servants in the seventeen rooms of Bayshill Court. Mrs Catherine Asquith and Mrs Isabel Lochhead, both in fourteen-roomed houses on Shurdington Road, may have been friends as they signed together. Mrs Asquith was a widow of independent means, while her friend Mrs Lochhead and her husband, both just 40, seemed to have been living on inherited money for many years.

The CUWFA also drew in signatories from more outlying areas. For example, Mr and Mrs Bagnall-Oakeley of Edgbaston House, Prestbury, Mrs Ada Cameron from Capp Mill House, Painswick, Miss Fanny Cameron of High Street, Chipping Campden,[2] who was living with her widowed mother, a doctor's wife, and Mr and Mrs Percy Cunynghame of Badgeworth, an early retiree from the Sarawak Civil Service. There were also the women from Alderton and Kemerton who emerged in the story of the Tewkesbury/Winchcombe WSS movement.

---

2   There was some WSS activity in Chipping Campden at the end of 1913, with a drawing-room meeting hosted by Mrs Mabel New, wife of a solicitor, at her home in the High Street. It was chaired by Lady Blomfield, whose two daughters were to cause a stir when one shouted out about the horror of forcible feeding when she was about to be presented to the king in June 1914. Lady Blomfield, the wife of an eminent architect, was based in Chelsea but had previously lived in Broadway. Grace Hadow of Cirencester went to help raise support, and in May 1914 it was announced that a branch had been formed with twenty-six members and thirty 'Friends' – a good start for a town of this size (CC 05/12/13 and 22/05/14).

One juicy tale emerged from some investigation of one CUWFA signatory. She was Mrs Charlotte Littler Downman, wife of Rev. Hugh Downman. They had been living in Cheltenham in 1901, but by 1911 were lodging in Great Malvern. However, in 1910, when a court case was brought against her, she was living in Royal Well Terrace, Cheltenham. A dressmaker brought a claim for non-payment, but she claimed she had been overcharged and was defended by Dr Earengey! Further investigation suggests that the couple were not scrupulous in their financial affairs – he had been declared bankrupt in 1899 while a clergyman in Northamptonshire, the furniture was then claimed by his wife, presumably in an attempt to evade confiscation. He then disappeared and it emerged that he had used the school funds for which he was treasurer for his own purposes! His appointment to the rectory of Grafton Fyford in Worcestershire in 1922 is surprising to say the least. All irrelevant to women's suffrage, except it was he who gave the vote of thanks at the presentation to James Agg-Gardner!

Sympathisers – What is exciting from this section is to see women emerging who would otherwise have remained hidden. The greatest revelation is the number of domestic servants who felt able to come forward. For example, we see Beatrice Nash, a parlourmaid to a retired Indian army officer in Charlton Kings, and Eva Driver, the cook to another ex-colonial household in Charlton Kings, who appear to have signed independently. On the other hand, we see households where domestic staff seem to have followed the lead of their employers: the Swiney household, for example, where the cook, parlourmaid and housemaid all signed together with the Swiney grandson, who was still at school. The household of the Jordan mother and two daughters (WSS) is similar where Henry Jordan, the head of the household, signed together with his cook and housemaid. Did the Swineys or the Jordans put pressure on their servants, or were their servants inspired by their example? If one worked for Mrs Swiney, one could not be unaware of her activities or of meetings held at the house, or the WSS summer garden parties in the grounds.

Signatures of the schoolboy grandson and servants of Major and Mrs Swiney. (D5130/6/6 by kind permission Gloucestershire Archives)

Signatures of a group of
working-class neighbours from
Moorend Road. (D5130/6/6
by kind permission
Gloucestershire Archives)

What made close neighbours from Ferndale Cottages, Moorend Road, go together to sign the book? Were they genuine supporters or were they persuaded by an employer? Both Mr and Mrs George Barnfield and Mrs Mary Ann and Miss Rosie Cross lived in small, four-roomed cottages: George Barnfield was a general labourer and Mrs Cross's husband was a domestic gardener, and Rose was a domestic nurse, aged only 16. In between their signatures is that of Mrs Matilda Bendall of Providence Row, Moorend Road, whose husband was a builder's labourer. This little knot of unskilled working-class neighbours either made a purposeful journey to some central point, or possibly had the book brought to them by some more influential person.

One strong occupational group emerges among the Sympathisers. There is a disproportionate number in the drapery business. Some of them were from Cavendish House, single men and women living in a hostel on the High Street, and the young Ernest Pollard was a porter living with many other employees on the shop premises. Others were living at home with parents or with wife and family. It is possible that there was someone orchestrating this support – Miss Ralph of Cavendish House had become WSPU treasurer in 1914, and Miss Gertrude Blandford who was temporarily WSPU secretary was a buyer for a draper in the town. There was male support in Lance's drapery store, as Mr Edgar Walmsley was a buyer for the establishment and signed the book. Even more important support came from the managing director, William Welstead, who perhaps wielded some power over his employees. The Conservative councillor Thomas Rees Jones was a draper, and had spoken in favour of women's suffrage in 1910 when he said it was absurd for women to be able to vote for the council but not for Parliament, when 'ladies' coachmen and gardeners enjoyed the latter privilege'.

Unlike in the three societies' representation, there are more lower middle-class and upper working-class men and women under the Sympathisers heading.

Shopkeepers such as ironmongers, fishmongers, dressmakers (not high-class costumiers such as Madame Gilmore of Montpellier or Miss Florence Long of Cambray), ladies' hairdressers, assistants in various shops (books, art products, jewellery, greengrocery, post office, children's outfitter), carpenter, manager of a motor garage, baker and confectioner all feature in the list. In addition, there are a female baths attendant, a jobbing gardener and a skin dresser in a tanyard, all unskilled occupations. It would have required some dedication from the above people to join a women's suffrage society and be certain that they could afford to do so. Moreover, many of them would have felt uneasy in the social settings which membership entailed.

When the organiser, Miss Kelley, wrote that most of the important people in the town signed as sympathisers, it is unclear whether she meant political or social leaders. However, some can be identified. Mayor Charles Margrett (a confectioner by trade) and his wife had long been sympathisers, sometimes appearing on WSS platforms, so it is not surprising that they were signatories. From the world of education came Thomas Whittard, who had run the private school The Hall, which was attended by tea dealer and grocer John How's daughters Florence (Earengey) and Edith (How-Martyn). Newspaper editor William Crawford signed, as did father John and son William Henry Banks who had their stationer's and bookseller's shop in the Promenade. Arthur Pruen, solicitor, was for a while the partner of Dr Earengey and his father had been a WSS supporter, so there were close links to pull him towards signing. John Alexander Matthews was a music professor at St Paul's College, a writer and editor who founded the Festival Musical Society, and was for many years the organist at St Matthew's Church.

Another group was male Conservative activists. Horace Doxsey, a teacher for the local authority, had been secretary of the local party, while Charles Pearce was club steward at the Conservative Club in Albion Street – his signature could have been an expedient move. The Moore brothers, Ernest and Willoughby, were big supporters and ran an influential building firm in the town. William Cypher had run the finances for the post-1911 by-election celebration party for Agg-Gardner, and owned the highly successful Cypher's Nursery on Queen's Road. Samuel Brooks of Sydenham Villas Road was a long-term Conservative activist and well-travelled journalist and writer.

Some oddities emerge. Mr Henry Foster of Lypiatt Road, who had a very lavish society wedding in Cheltenham in 1902, had been living and working in Argentina as a rancher, so the reason for his support is not immediately obvious. Mrs Edith Maitland was the wife of a retired 'Gentleman of the King's Bodyguard for Scotland' and was living in sixteen-roomed luxury in Old Bath Road with her husband and a

```
ESTABLISHED 1868.
————
E. W. & W. J. MOORE,
Builders & Sanitary Engineers.
HIGH-CLASS DECORATORS.
House Repairs in all its branches.
BATH PARADE, BATH ROAD
and GRATTON ROAD.
————
TELEPHONE 215.
```

An advertisement for the Moore brothers' firm. They were both Conservative activists and signed the book as 'Sympathisers'. (*Looker-On*, various editions)

nephew who was mining for gold in California – and two servants! As her husband was 70, he would have served in the Queen's Household in Scotland before 1901, but his wife obviously did not agree with Queen Victoria's views on the subject, which had been made known in her attack on Lady Amberley in Stroud (see Chapter 2)!

As in the CUWFA, a few signatories were drawn from outside the town, but were not complete outsiders like those who signed for the WFL. For example, Nellie Adelaide Mason was living in High Street, Winchcombe and assisting her grandmother in her grocery business, while Mrs Grace Healing made the short journey from Avonside, Tewkesbury, where her husband was a prosperous flour miller. A shorter step was from Staverton where Emily Jarvis, the wife of the Free Church minister, lived, as did Mary McIlquham, the daughter of Mrs Harriet McIlquham who had done so much to establish the movement in Cheltenham. This support from outside Cheltenham is not surprising – both the MPs for Tewkesbury and Stroud voted against the bill which Agg-Gardner had sponsored.

What this book has given is invaluable. It has provided an insight into the women's suffrage movement which can reveal the layers of support it had in one locality. It has enabled a large database to be set up to share with anyone interested – a resource which can be expanded with information from anyone else: tinyurl.com/cotswoldsuffrage

This is the stuff of which local history is made …

What happened to these women's hopes and aspirations? All the men who signed this book would be granted the vote in 1918 if they did not already have it. But many of the women would remain without a vote until 1928. The Act of 1918 only gave the vote to women over 30 who were householders or married to householders, or rented property for an annual charge of £5 or more, or were graduates.

This meant that many activists who were unmarried daughters living with their parents would not qualify. Brave Nellie Mason who made the journey from Winchcombe to sign would not have qualified, as she lived with her grandparents. The domestic servants in the household of Mrs Swiney, who had fought for the vote for so long, would not qualify. In spite of their courageous campaign, women had not yet gained full recognition. That had to wait for further male enlightenment!

Index

Numbers in italic indicates illustration